COME
UNTO
CHRIST

COME
UNTO
CHRIST

Ezra Taft Benson

Deseret Book Company   Salt Lake City, Utah

©1983 Deseret Book Company
All rights reserved
Printed in the United States of America
ISBN 0-87747-997-6
First printing December 1983
Second printing February 1984

Contents

Preface

When I was young, I belonged to the Whitney Ward in Whitney, Idaho. The ward was not large. It had approximately three hundred members, most of whom were faithful Church members. I recall, as a young boy, learning the gospel from the older members who had been "through the fire." I can still see their intent faces and hear their fervent testimonies, which were a great source of strength to me.

The members of that ward were doing what faithful Saints in all ages have done; to use the apostle Peter's phrase, they were "ready always to give . . . a reason of the hope" that was in them. (1 Peter 3:15.)

Today some question the divinity of the Lord Jesus Christ. Others who profess to follow Him claim unwittingly that The Church of Jesus Christ of Latter-day Saints is a non-Christian organization since we do not agree in all points of doctrine with historical, traditional Christianity.

I therefore deem it expedient to declare my conviction

and belief about the Lord Jesus Christ or, like those who have preceded me, to give reason for the hope that is in me.

I offer at least five fundamental reasons to demonstrate why members of The Church of Jesus Christ of Latter-day Saints are Christian in every sense of the word.

First: We believe that Jesus Christ is divine. We do not qualify the term *divinity*. We believe Jesus Christ to be God's Only Begotten Son in the flesh. We believe He is, as the name implies, the Anointed One—the Promised Messiah.

The marks of His divinity are explained in chapter one, "What Think We of Christ."

Second: We believe the teachings of Jesus. We accept His admonitions and instructions as being binding on the entire human family. Indeed, we affirm that one cannot enter the kingdom of heaven without compliance to the laws and ordinances prescribed by Him, the great Lawgiver.

These teachings are discussed in chapters two through nine.

Third: We believe that Jesus Christ has restored His church on earth today. This church bears all the hallmarks of the original church—apostolic authority, ordinances, and gifts of the Holy Spirit. This restoration of authority and power was necessitated by a universal apostasy that removed the apostolic power from His original church. Indeed, to His own generation, Jesus prophesied, "The kingdom of God shall be taken from you, and given to a nation bringing forth the fruits thereof." (Matthew 21:43.)

Chapters ten and eleven explain the restoration of His church and its prophesied destiny.

Fourth: After the restoration of His church in modern times, Jesus Christ named His church. With impeccable logic, He inquired of a former generation, "How be it my church save it be called in my name? . . . if it be called in the name of a man then it be the church of a man." (Book of Mormon,

3 Nephi 27:8.) Thus by revelation in our day, He named His church—even "The Church of Jesus Christ of Latter-day Saints." (See Doctrine and Covenants 115:4.) Since we accept His church as the kingdom of God on earth, we are under obligation, as His disciples, to preach His gospel to all the world and to emulate the standards of His teachings to all men.

Chapters twelve and thirteen discuss some of the expectations of members of His church.

Fifth: We believe that Jesus Christ will come again as our resurrected Lord and Master to reign as King of kings and Lord of lords. Then He will cleanse the earth and establish His millennial reign on earth.

Our hope in these future events is discussed in chapters fourteen and fifteen.

Last: I offer as a conclusion to this volume (chapter sixteen) my own testimony as one of His appointed special witnesses in this day.

I urge all to do as the title of this book invites—*come unto Christ*. Yes, "come unto Christ, and be perfected in him, and deny yourselves of all ungodliness; . . . and love God with all your might, mind and strength." Then "is his grace sufficient for you, that by his grace ye may be perfect in Christ." (Book of Mormon, Moroni 10:32.)

Come unto Christ, because "he inviteth . . . all to come unto him and partake of his goodness; and he denieth none that come unto him, black and white, bond and free, male and female; . . . all are alike unto [Him]." (Book of Mormon, 2 Nephi 26:33.)

The author wishes to make clear that this is not a Church publication, and the opinions and views expressed by him in this publication are those for which he alone is responsible.

Chapter One

What Think We of Christ?

There is none other name under heaven given among men, whereby we must be saved. (Acts 4:12)

The apostle Matthew gives an account of Jesus responding to the Sadducees, who claimed there was no resurrection. Jesus silenced them with His answer. Hearing that the Sadducees had been subdued, the Pharisees tempted Jesus with a question from one of their own: "Master, which is the great commandment in the law?"

Jesus replied, "Thou shalt love the Lord thy God with all thy heart, and with all thy soul, and with all thy mind. This is the first and great commandment. And the second is like unto it, Thou shalt love thy neighbour as thyself. On these two commandments hang all the law and the prophets."

Then Jesus turned to the Pharisees and questioned them: "What think ye of Christ? whose son is he?" (Matthew 22: 36-42.)

1

Several years ago, a number of prominent theologians were asked the question, What do you think of Jesus? Their replies startled many professed Christians.

One asserted that a "true Christian" must reject the resurrection. Another admitted that New Testament scholars were so divided on the question that one cannot say anything certain about the historical Jesus. Another scholar and teacher of Jesuit priests explained, "It is difficult to say in our age what the divinity of Jesus can mean. We are groping now for a way to express it—we just don't know." ("Easter 1966—A Quest for the True Jesus," *Newsweek,* April 11, 1966, p. 72.)

In a public opinion poll conducted by George Gallup, Jr., seven in ten adult American respondents said they believed in the divinity of Christ. But 90 percent of these said that Jesus is divine only in the sense that He embodies the best that is in all men. (*Church News,* October 23, 1983.)

The Church of Jesus Christ of Latter-day Saints consents to no such ambiguity in relation to our position regarding Jesus Christ.

The following marks of His divinity are fundamental truths about our Lord that we believe must be accepted if we truly consider ourselves His disciples.

Jesus Is Divine Because of His Divine Birth

The most fundamental doctrine of true Christianity is the divine birth of the child Jesus. This doctrine is not generally comprehended by the world. The paternity of Jesus Christ is one of the "mysteries of godliness" comprehended only by the spiritually-minded.

The apostle Matthew recorded: "Now the birth of Jesus Christ was on this wise: When as his mother Mary was espoused to Joseph, before they came together, she was found with child of the Holy Ghost." (Matthew 1:18.)

Luke rendered a plainer meaning to the divine conception. He quoted the angel Gabriel's words to Mary: "The Holy

Ghost shall come upon thee, and *the power of the Highest shall overshadow thee:* therefore also that holy [being] which shall be born of thee shall be called the Son of God." (Luke 1:35; italics added.)

Some six hundred years before Jesus was born, an ancient prophet had a vision. He saw Mary and described her as "a virgin, most beautiful and fair above all other virgins." He then saw her "carried away in the Spirit . . . for the space of a time." When she returned, she was "bearing a child in her arms . . . even the Son of the Eternal Father." (Book of Mormon, 1 Nephi 11:15, 19-21.)

Thus the testimonies of appointed witnesses leave no question as to the paternity of Jesus Christ. God was the Father of Jesus' mortal tabernacle, and Mary, a mortal woman, was His mother. He is therefore the only person born who rightfully deserves the title "the *Only* Begotten Son of God."

From the time of Christ's heaven-heralded birth, heresies have crept into Christianity intended to dilute or undermine the pure doctrines of the gospel. These heresies, by and large, are sponsored by the philosophies of men and, in many instances, advocated by so-called Christian scholars. Their intent is to make Christianity more palatable, more reasonable, and so they attempt to humanize Jesus and give natural explanations to those things which are divine.

An example is Jesus' birth. The so-called scholars seek to convince us that the divine birth of Christ as proclaimed in the New Testament was not divine at all and that Mary was not a virgin at the time of Jesus' conception. They would have us believe that Joseph, the foster-father of Jesus, was His physical father, and that therefore Jesus was human in all attributes and characteristics. They appear generous in their praise of Him when they say that He was a great moral philosopher, perhaps even the greatest. But the import of their effort is to repudiate the divine Sonship of Jesus, for on that doctrine rest all other claims of Christianity.

The Church of Jesus Christ of Latter-day Saints proclaims that Jesus Christ is the Son of God in the most literal sense. The body in which He performed His mission in the flesh was sired by that same Holy Being we worship as God, our Eternal Father. Jesus was not the son of Joseph, nor was He begotten by the Holy Ghost. He is the Son of the Eternal Father!

Jesus Is Divine Because of His Ministry

The entire ministry of the Master was characterized by His voluntary subordination to His Heavenly Father's will: "For I came down from heaven, not to do mine own will, but the will of him that sent me." (John 6:38.)

As the Messiah, He fully understood His atoning mission and the will of His Father. He testified:

"My Father sent me that I might be lifted up upon the cross. . . . that I might draw all men unto me. . . .

"Therefore, according to the power of the Father I will draw all men unto me, that they may be judged according to their works.

"And it shall come to pass, that whoso repenteth and is baptized in my name shall be filled; and if he endureth to the end, behold, him will I hold guiltless before my Father at that day when I shall stand to judge the world." (Book of Mormon, 3 Nephi 27:14-16.)

He came to restore the fulness of a gospel that had been lost by apostasy. He came not to repeal Moses, but to subordinate Mosaic law to the higher law of Christ. In order that His own people would know that He had authority to do so, He proclaimed His Messiahship with words and metaphors that they could not mistake:

"I am that bread of life." (John 6:48.)

"I am the good shepherd." (John 10:14.)

"I am the light of the world." (John 8:12.)

"I am the resurrection, and the life." (John 11:25.)

"I am the way, the truth, and the life." (John 14:6.)

The hallmark of His ministry, as prophets before Him testified that it would be, was many mighty miracles: "healing the sick, raising the dead, causing the lame to walk, the blind to receive their sight, and the deaf to hear, and curing all manner of diseases." (Book of Mormon, Mosiah 3:5.)

One of the greatest of these miracles was the raising of His friend Lazarus from the dead. You remember how, when He received word that Lazarus was sick, He deliberately delayed going to Bethany to minister to His friend.

The custom among the Jews was to bury their deceased on the same day of death; they held a superstition that the spirit lingered around the body for three days and then departed on the fourth day. Jesus was very familiar with their beliefs, and He therefore delayed His arrival in Bethany until Lazarus had been in the grave for four days. In that way there would be no question about the miracle He was to perform.

As the Savior approached Bethany, He was met by Martha, a sister of Lazarus. She said, "Lord, if thou hadst been here, my brother had not died."

Jesus said, "Thy brother shall rise again."

Not understanding, Martha replied, "I know that he shall rise again in the resurrection at the last day."

Then Jesus proclaimed: "I am the resurrection, and the life: he that believeth in me, though he were dead, yet shall he live: and whosoever liveth and believeth in me shall never die."

Jesus was then taken to the place of burial, a cave with a stone in front. He commanded the mourners to remove the stone, after which He offered up a prayer to His Father. He then cried in a loud voice, "Lazarus, come forth." Here is the apostle John's record of what took place: "And he that was dead came forth, bound hand and foot with graveclothes: and his face was bound about with a napkin." (See John 11: 1-44.)

This miracle was such irrefutable proof of the Messiahship of Jesus that the Sanhedrin determined Jesus must die, for, they said, He "doeth many miracles" that will cause the people to believe. (See John 11:47.)

Sadly, however, John also recorded: "Though he had done so many miracles before them, yet they [the people] believed not on him." (John 12:37.)

Today some unbelievers among us spread seeds of heresy, claiming that Jesus could not cast out evil spirits and did not walk on water nor heal the sick nor miraculously feed five thousand nor calm storms nor raise the dead. These would have us believe that such claims are fantastic and that there is a natural explanation for each alleged miracle. Some have gone so far as to publish psychological explanations for His reported miracles. But Jesus' entire ministry was a mark of His divinity. He spoke as God, He acted as God, and He performed works that only God Himself can do. His works bear testimony to His divinity.

Jesus Is Divine Because of His Great Atoning Sacrifice

Were it not for the power that Jesus inherited from His Father, His great atonement would not have been possible.

On the night Jesus was betrayed, He took three of the Twelve and went into the place called Gethsemane. There He suffered the pains of all men, which suffering, He said, "caused myself, even God, the greatest of all, to tremble because of pain, and to bleed at every pore, and to suffer both body and spirit—and would that I might not drink the bitter cup, and shrink." (Doctrine and Covenants 19:18.)

In spite of that excruciating ordeal, He took the cup and drank! He suffered as only God could suffer, bearing our griefs, carrying our sorrows, being wounded for our transgressions, voluntarily submitting Himself to the iniquity of us all, just as Isaiah prophesied. (See Isaiah 53:4-6.)

It was in Gethsemane that Jesus took on Himself the sins of the world, in Gethsemane that His pain was equivalent to the cumulative burden of all men, in Gethsemane that He descended below all things so that all could repent and come to Him.

The mortal mind fails to fathom, the tongue cannot express, the pen of man cannot describe the breadth, the depth, the height of the suffering of our Lord—nor His infinite love for us.

Yet there are those who arrogantly declare the most pernicious heresy: that the blood which extruded from the physical body of our Lord on that night had no efficacy for the redemption of man. They would have us believe that the only significance to Gethsemane was that Jesus made His decision there to go to the cross. They say that any suffering Jesus endured was only personal, not redemptive for the whole human race. I know of no heresy more destructive to faith than this, for the individual who so accepts this delusion is beguiled to believe that he can achieve salvation on the basis of his own merit, intelligence, and personal effort.

We must never forget that "by grace are ye saved through faith; and that not of yourselves: it is the gift of God: not of works, lest any man should boast." (Ephesians 2:8-9.)

As a church, we are in accord with an ancient prophet who said, "It is by grace that we are saved, after all we can do." (Book of Mormon, 2 Nephi 25:23.) Grace consists of God's gift to His children wherein He gave His Only Begotten Son in order that whosoever would believe in Him and comply with His laws and ordinances would have everlasting life.

By grace, the Savior accomplished His atoning sacrifice so that all mankind will attain immortality.

By His grace and by our faith in His atonement and our

repentance of our sins, we receive the strength to do the necessary works that we otherwise could not do by our own power.

By His grace, we receive an endowment of blessing and spiritual strength that may eventually lead us to eternal life if we endure to the end.

By His grace, we become more like His divine personality.

Yes, it is "by grace that we are saved, after all we can do." What is meant by the phrase "after all we can do"?

"After all we can do" includes extending our best effort.

"After all we can do" includes living His commandments.

"After all we can do" includes loving our fellowmen and praying for those who regard us as their adversary.

"After all we can do" means clothing the naked, feeding the hungry, visiting the sick, and giving "succor [to] those that stand in need of [our] succor" (Mosiah 4:16), remembering that what we do unto one of the least of God's children, we do unto Him (Matthew 25:40).

"After all we can do" means leading chaste, clean, pure lives, being scrupulously honest in all our dealings, and treating others the way we would want to be treated.

As I contemplate the glorious atonement of our Lord, which extended from Gethsemane to Golgotha, I am led to exclaim with reverence and gratitude:

I stand all amazed at the love Jesus offers me,
Confused at the grace that so fully he proffers me;
I tremble to know that for me he was crucified,
That for me a sinner, he suffered, he bled and died.

I marvel that he would descend from his throne divine
To rescue a soul so rebellious and proud as mine;
That He should extend his great love unto such as I,
Sufficient to own, to redeem, and to justify.

Oh, it is wonderful that he should care for me,
Enough to die for me!
Oh, it is wonderful, wonderful to me!

—*Hymns,* no. 80

Jesus Is Divine Because of His Literal Resurrection

I have stood in reverent awe at the Garden Tomb in Jerusalem. It is history's most significant tomb—because it is empty!

On the third day following His burial, Jesus came forth. The empty tomb was the cause of consternation to His disciples and others in Jerusalem.

He appeared first to Mary Magdalene. He approached her as she was weeping in the garden and said, "Woman, why weepest thou? whom seekest thou?"

Mary, who supposed that the gardener was speaking, said, "Sir, if thou have borne him hence, tell me where thou hast laid him, and I will take him away."

Jesus then said, "Mary."

She now recognized His voice and exclaimed, "Rabboni," or in other words, "Master." (John 20:15-17.)

Of all the marks of Jesus' divinity, none has greater support by the testimony of eyewitnesses than His literal, bodily resurrection:

Several women testified that they saw Him alive.

Two disciples on the road to Emmaus dined with Him.

Peter proclaimed himself an eyewitness to the resurrection.

There were many special appearances of the risen Lord to the Twelve.

In addition to these testimonies, over five hundred saw Him at one time.

Paul certified that he saw the resurrected Lord.

Since the day of resurrection when Jesus became the "firstfruits of them that slept" (1 Corinthians 15:20), there have been those who disbelieve and scoff. They maintain there is no life beyond mortal existence. Some have even written books that contain their fanciful heresies to suggest how Jesus' disciples perpetrated the hoax of His resurrection.

I give you my testimony: The resurrection of Jesus Christ is the greatest historical event in the world to date.

He lives! He lives with a resurrected body. There is no truth nor fact of which I am more assured than the truth of the literal resurrection of our Lord.

What think we of Christ? Whose Son is He?

We accept Him as the divine Son of God.

We believe Him to be the promised Messiah.

We rely on His atonement for personal salvation.

We declare His literal bodily resurrection.

Yes, we believe in Jesus Christ, but more. We look to Him, we trust Him, and we strive to emulate His attributes because there has not been, nor will there ever be, any "other name given nor any other way nor means whereby salvation can come unto the children of men, only in and through the name of Christ, the Lord Omnipotent." (Mosiah 3:17.)

Chapter Two

Be Valiant in the Testimony of Jesus

We bear record—for we saw and heard . . . concerning them who shall come forth in the resurrection of the just—They are they who received the testimony of Jesus, and believed on his name and were baptized after the manner of his burial, . . . and who overcome by faith. (Doctrine and Covenants 76:50-51, 53)

A most priceless blessing available to every member of the Church is a testimony of the divinity of Jesus Christ and His church. A testimony is one of the few possessions we may take with us when we leave this life. Let me explain what it means to have a testimony of Jesus.

To have a testimony of Jesus is to possess knowledge through the Holy Ghost of the divine mission of Jesus Christ.

A testimony of Jesus is to know the divine nature of our

11

Lord's birth—that He is indeed the Only Begotten Son of God in the flesh.

A testimony of Jesus is to know that He was the promised Messiah and that while He sojourned among men He accomplished many mighty miracles.

A testimony of Jesus is to know that the laws He prescribed as His doctrine are true and then to abide by those laws and ordinances.

A testimony of Jesus is to know that He voluntarily took upon Himself the sins of all mankind in the Garden of Gethsemane, which caused Him to suffer in both body and spirit and to bleed from every pore. All this He did so that we would not have to suffer, if we would repent. (See Doctrine and Covenants 19:16, 18.)

A testimony of Jesus is to know that He came forth triumphantly from the grave with a physical, resurrected body. And because He lives, so shall all mankind.

A testimony of Jesus is to know that God the Father and His Son, Jesus Christ, did indeed appear to the Prophet Joseph Smith to establish a new dispensation of His gospel so that salvation may be preached to all nations before He comes.

A testimony of Jesus is to know that the church He established in the meridian of time and restored in modern times is, as the Lord has declared, "the only true and living church upon the face of the whole earth." (Doctrine and Covenants 1:30.)

A testimony of Jesus is to receive the words of His servants, the prophets, for as He has said, "Whether by mine own voice or by the voice of my servants, it is the same." (Doctrine and Covenants 1:38.)

A testimony of Jesus means that we accept the divine mission of Jesus Christ, embrace His gospel, and do His works. It means we accept the prophetic mission of Joseph Smith and his successors.

Speaking of those who will eventually receive the blessings of the celestial kingdom, the Lord said to Joseph Smith: "They are they who received the testimony of Jesus, and believed on his name and were baptized after the manner of his burial, being buried in the water in his name, and this according to the commandment which he has given." (Doctrine and Covenants 76:51.)

These are they who are valiant in their testimony of Jesus, who, as the Lord has declared, "overcome by faith, and are sealed by the Holy Spirit of promise, which the Father sheds forth upon all those who are just and true." (Doctrine and Covenants 76:53.)

"Those who are just and true." What an apt expression for those valiant in the testimony of Jesus! These are members of the Church who magnify their callings in the Church (see Doctrine and Covenants 84:33), pay their tithes and offerings, live morally clean lives, sustain their Church leaders by word and action, keep the Sabbath as a holy day, and obey all the commandments of God. They are courageous in defending truth and righteousness. To these the Lord has promised that "all thrones and dominions, principalities and powers, shall be revealed and set forth upon all who have endured valiantly for the gospel of Jesus Christ." (Doctrine and Covenants 121:29.)

Concerning those who will receive the terrestrial, or lesser, kingdom, the Lord said, "These are they who are not valiant in the testimony of Jesus; wherefore, they obtain not the crown over the kingdom of our God." (Doctrine and Covenants 76:79.) Not to be valiant in one's testimony is a tragedy of eternal consequence. These are members who know that this latter-day work is true but who fail to endure to the end. Some may even hold temple recommends, but they do not magnify their callings in the Church. Without valor, they do not take an affirmative stand for the kingdom of God. Some seek the praise, adulation, and honors of men; others attempt

to conceal their sins; and a few criticize those who preside
over them.

Considering some of the challenges that the Church cur-
rently faces and that it will continue to face in the future,
three statements of former Church leaders are especially significant.

President Joseph F. Smith said, "There are at least three
dangers that threaten the Church within. . . . They are flattery
of prominent men in the world, false educational ideas, and
sexual impurity." (*Gospel Doctrine,* Deseret Book, 1977, pp.
312-13.) These three dangers are of greater concern today
than when they were identified by President Smith.

A second statement is a prophecy by Heber C. Kimball,
counselor to President Brigham Young. Speaking to members of the Church who had come to the Salt Lake Valley, he
declared:

> To meet the difficulties that are coming, it will be necessary for
> you to have a knowledge of the truth of this work for yourselves.
> The difficulties will be of such a character that the man or woman
> who does not possess this personal knowledge or witness will fall.
> If you have not got the testimony, live right and call upon the Lord
> and cease not till you obtain it. If you do not you will not stand. . . .
> The time will come when no man nor woman will be able to
> endure on borrowed light. Each will have to be guided by the light
> within himself. . . . If you don't have it you will not stand; therefore
> seek for the testimony of Jesus and cleave to it, that when the trying
> time comes you may not stumble and fall. (Orson F. Whitney, *Life
> of Heber C. Kimball,* Stevens & Wallace, 1945, p. 450.)

A third statement is from President Harold B. Lee, my
boyhood companion and friend, and the eleventh president
of the Church:

> We have some tight places to go before the Lord is through
> with this church and the world in this dispensation, which is the
> last dispensation, which shall usher in the coming of the Lord. The
> gospel was restored to prepare a people ready to receive him. The

power of Satan will increase; we see it in evidence on every hand. There will be inroads within the Church. . . . We will see those who profess membership but secretly are plotting and trying to lead people not to follow the leadership that the Lord has set up to preside in this church.

Now the only safety we have as members of this church is to do exactly what the Lord said to the Church in that day when the Church was organized. We must learn to give heed to the words and commandments that the Lord shall give through his prophet, "as he receiveth them, walking . . . in all patience and faith." (Doctrine and Covenants 21:4-5.) There will be some things that take patience and faith. You may not like what comes from the authority of the Church. . . . But if you listen to these things, as if from the mouth of the Lord himself, with patience and faith, the promise is that "the gates of hell shall not prevail against you; yea, and the Lord God will disperse the powers of darkness from before you, and cause the heavens to shake for your good, and his name's glory." (Doctrine and Covenants 21:6.) (*Conference Report,* October 1970, p. 152.)

It seems to me that we have within these three prophetic statements the counsel necessary to stay valiant in our testimony of Jesus and the work of His church in these troubled times. One who rationalizes that he or she has a testimony of Jesus Christ but cannot accept direction and counsel from the leadership of His church is in a fundamentally unsound position and is in jeopardy of losing exaltation.

Some want to expose the weaknesses of Church leaders in an effort to show that they too are subject to human frailties and error like unto themselves. The danger of this questionable philosophy is illustrated by the following experience.

President Brigham Young revealed that on one occasion he was tempted to be critical of the Prophet Joseph Smith regarding a certain financial matter. He said that the feeling did not last for more than perhaps thirty seconds. That feeling, he said, caused him great sorrow in his heart. The lesson he gave to members of the Church in his day may well be increased in significance today because the devil continues more active. He said:

> I clearly saw and understood, *by the spirit of revelation manifested to me,* that if I was to harbor a thought in my heart that Joseph could be wrong in anything, I would begin to lose confidence in him, and that feeling would grow from step to step, and from one degree to another, until at last I would have the same lack of confidence in his being the mouthpiece of the Almighty. . . .
>
> I repented of my unbelief, and that too, very suddenly; I repented about as quickly as I committed the error. It was not for me to question whether Joseph was dictated by the Lord at all times and under all circumstances. . . .
>
> It was not my prerogative to call him in question with regard to any act of his life. He was God's servant, and not mine. He did not belong to the people but to the Lord, and was doing the work of the Lord. (*Journal of Discourses* 4:297; italics added.)

Let us be valiant in our testimony of Jesus all the days of our lives. Let our valiancy be reflected by our actions. Therefore we must—

Seek a witness by the Holy Ghost that Jesus Christ is the Son of God and has restored His church on earth today.

Study His gospel, thereby "feasting upon the word of Christ." (Book of Mormon, 2 Nephi 31:20.)

Sustain His servants whom He has appointed to preside in His church.

Love our fellowmen and seek to serve them.

Chapter Three

Seek the Spirit

When the Comforter is come, . . . even the Spirit of truth, . . . he shall testify of me. (John 15:26)

Several years after Joseph Smith was martyred, he appeared to President Brigham Young. His message for the Saints at that time constitutes the theme of this chapter:

"Tell the people to be humble and faithful, and be sure to keep the spirit of the Lord and it will lead them right. Be careful and not turn away the still small voice; it will teach you what to do and where to go; it will yield the fruits of the kingdom. Tell the brethren to keep their hearts open to conviction, so that when the Holy Ghost comes to them, their hearts will be ready to receive it." (*Manuscript History of Brigham Young,* February 23, 1847.)

The most important thing in our work in the Church of Jesus Christ is the Spirit. I have always felt that. We must remain open and sensitive to the promptings of the Holy Ghost in this work as well as in all other aspects of our lives.

Bishop John Wells, a former member of the Presiding Bishopric, was a great detail man and was responsible for many Church reports. President David O. McKay and President Harold B. Lee used to relate an experience from his life that is instructive to all of us.

A son of Bishop and Sister Wells was killed in a railroad accident in Emigration Canyon, east of Salt Lake City. He was run over by a freight car. Sister Wells could not be consoled. She received no comfort during the funeral and continued her mourning after her son was laid to rest. Bishop Wells feared for her health, as she was in a state of deep anguish.

One day, soon after the funeral, Sister Wells was lying on her bed in a state of mourning. The son appeared to her and said, "Mother, do not mourn, do not cry. I am all right." He then related to her how the accident took place. Apparently there had been some question—even suspicion—about the accident, because the young man was an experienced railroad man. But he told his mother that it was clearly an accident.

He also told her that as soon as he realized that he was in another sphere, he had tried to reach his father but could not. His father was so busy with the details of his office and work that he could not respond to the promptings. Therefore, the son had come to his mother. He then said, "Tell Father that all is well with me, and I want you not to mourn anymore."

President McKay used this experience to teach that we must always be responsive to the whisperings of the Spirit. These promptings come most often when we are not under the pressure of appointments and when we are not caught up in the worries of day-to-day life.

To have the Spirit in our lives, we should take time to meditate.

Meditation on a passage of scripture—James 1:5—led a young boy into a grove of trees to commune with his

Heavenly Father. That is what opened the heavens in this dispensation.

Meditation on a passage of scripture from the book of John in the New Testament brought forth the great revelation on the three degrees of glory.

Meditation on another passage of scripture from the First Epistle of Peter opened the heavens to President Joseph F. Smith, and he saw the spirit world. That revelation, known as the Vision of the Redemption of the Dead, is now a part of the Doctrine and Covenants.

We should ponder the meaning of the work in which we are engaged. The Lord has counseled, "Let the solemnities of eternity rest upon your minds." (Doctrine and Covenants 43:34.) We cannot do that when our minds are preoccupied with the cares of the world.

We should read and study the scriptures. Everything we learn in the holy places, the temples, is based on the scriptures. These teachings are what the scriptures refer to as the "mysteries of godliness." They are to be comprehended by the power of the Holy Ghost, for the Lord has given this promise to His faithful and obedient servants: "Thou mayest know the mysteries and peaceable things." (Doctrine and Covenants 42:61.)

A statement by President Spencer W. Kimball illustrates how we may develop more spirituality in our lives: "I find that when I get casual in my relationship with divinity and when it seems that no divine ear is listening and no divine voice is speaking, that I am far, far away. If I immerse myself in the scriptures the distance narrows and the spirituality returns. I find myself loving more intensely those whom I must love with all my heart and mind and strength, and loving them more I find it easier to abide their counsel." (Address to Seminary and Institute Personnel, Brigham Young University, July 11, 1966.)

That is great counsel that I know by experience to be true.

The more we are familiar with the scriptures, the closer we become to the mind and will of the Lord. It will be easier for us to allow the truths of eternity to rest on our minds.

We should ponder matters that we do not understand. The Lord commanded Oliver Cowdery, "Study it out in your mind; then you must ask me if it be right, and if it is right I will cause that your bosom shall burn within you; therefore, *you shall feel that it is right.*" (Doctrine and Covenants 9:8; italics added.)

We hear the words of the Lord most often by a feeling. If we are humble and sensitive, the Lord will prompt us through our feelings. That is why spiritual promptings move us on occasion to great joy, sometimes to tears. Many times my emotions have been made tender and my feelings very sensitive when touched by the Spirit.

The Holy Ghost causes our feelings to be more tender. We feel more charitable and compassionate. We are calmer. We have a greater capacity to love. People want to be around us because our very countenances radiate the influence of the Spirit. We are more godly in character. As a result, we are more sensitive to the promptings of the Holy Ghost and thus able to comprehend spiritual things.

We should take to heart the words of the Savior: "Treasure up in your minds *continually* the words of life." (Doctrine and Covenants 84:85; italics added.)

My wife's mother, Barbara Smith Amussen, was an officiator in the Logan Temple for twenty years, a widow for forty years, and a woman without guile. I loved her so much that I spent a lot of time with her, because she was a widow and there was no priesthood in the home. In fact, I spent so much time with her that some of my own friends accused me of courting the mother rather than her daughter. She would often make notes of questions as she read the scriptures, and then we would discuss those questions together.

This choice woman knew the exact time she was to depart mortal life. Her husband, a Danish convert and Utah's first pioneer jeweler and watchmaker, Carl Christian Amussen, appeared to her in either a dream or a vision. She admitted, "I'm not sure which, but it was so real it seemed that he was right in the room. He said he had come to tell me that my time in mortal life was ending and that on the following Thursday [it was then Friday], I would be expected to leave mortal life."

Her oldest daughter, Mabel, said, "Oh, Mother, you've been worrying about something. You've not been feeling well."

Her mother replied, "Everything's fine. I feel wonderful. There's nothing to worry about. I just know I'll be leaving next Thursday." Then she added, "Mabel, when the time comes, I'd like to pass away in your home in the upper room where I used to sit and tell the boys Book of Mormon and Church history stories when they were little fellows."

As the time drew near, she attended fast meeting in her ward. The bishop told us she stood and talked as though she were going on a long journey. "She was bidding us all goodbye," said the bishop, "expressing her love for us and the joy that had been hers working in the temple, which was just a few yards away from the chapel." And then she bore a fervent testimony.

The bishop was so impressed that, following her testimony, he arose and announced the closing song, although the ward members had not been together quite an hour.

As the days passed, she went to the bank, drew out her small savings, paid all her bills, and went to Bishop Hall's mortuary and picked out her casket. Then she had the water and the power turned off in her home and went down to Mabel's. The day before she passed away, her son came to visit her. They sat by the bed and held hands as they talked.

On the day of her passing, Mabel came into the room where her mother was reclining on the bed. Her mother said, "Mabel, I feel a little bit drowsy. I feel I will go to sleep. Do not disturb me if I sleep until the eventide."

Those were her last words, and she peacefully passed away.

Spirituality—being in tune with the Spirit of the Lord—is the greatest need of Latter-day Saints. We should strive for the constant companionship of the Holy Ghost all the days of our lives. When we have the Spirit, we will love to serve, we will love the Lord, and we will love those whom we serve.

Spiritual-mindedness does not come without effort. We live in a very wicked world. We are surrounded with propaganda that evil is good and good is evil. False teachings abound that affect us. Almost everything that is wholesome, good, pure, uplifting, and strengthening is being challenged as never before.

One reason we are on this earth is to discern between truth and error. This discernment comes by the Holy Ghost, not just our intellectual faculties.

When we earnestly and honestly seek for the truth, this beautiful promise finds fulfillment: "God shall give unto you knowledge by his Holy Spirit, yea, by the unspeakable gift of the Holy Ghost." (Doctrine and Covenants 121:26.)

We live in a time when the devil is on the loose and is working among the Saints to thwart and tear down the work of God. But he will not succeed. Individuals may fall and there may be those who betray sacred covenants, but the kingdom of God will roll forward until it reaches its decreed destiny to fill the entire earth.

I carry in my calendar book a passage of scripture that I sometimes use to remind myself and others about the eventual outcome of efforts to destroy the Church: "No weapon that is formed against thee shall prosper; and every tongue that shall revile against thee in judgment thou shalt condemn. This is the heritage of the servants of the Lord, and their righteousness is of me, saith the Lord." (Book of Mormon, 3 Nephi 22:17.)

The Lord has prospered this work and will continue to do so. He is close to His servants, even within whispering distance of heaven.

While incarcerated in the Liberty Jail, the Prophet Joseph Smith eloquently wrote:

"The things of God are of deep import; and time, and experience, and careful and ponderous and solemn thoughts can only find them out. Thy mind, O man! if thou wilt lead a soul unto salvation, must stretch as high as the utmost heavens, and search into and contemplate the darkest abyss—*thou must commune with God.* How much more dignified and noble are the thoughts of God, than the vain imaginations of the human heart! None but fools will trifle with the souls of men." (*History of the Church* 3:295; italics added.)

This latter-day work is spiritual. It takes spirituality to comprehend it, to love it, and to discern it. Therefore, we should seek the Spirit in all we do. That is our challenge.

Chapter Four

Pray Always

Pray always, and I will pour out my Spirit upon you, and great shall be your blessing—yea, even more than if you should obtain treasures of earth. (Doctrine and Covenants 19:38)

During His earthly ministry, Jesus taught us a pattern for prayer:

After this manner therefore pray ye: Our Father which art in heaven, Hallowed be thy name.

Thy kingdom come. Thy will be done in earth, as it is in heaven.

Give us this day our daily bread.

And forgive us our debts, as we forgive our debtors.

And lead us not into temptation, but deliver us from evil: For thine is the kingdom, and the power, and the glory, for ever. Amen. (Matthew 6:9-13.)

He further instructed: "Men ought always to pray, and not to faint." (Luke 18:1.)

"Watch and pray," He said, "that ye enter not into tempta-tion." (Matthew 26:41.)

In this dispensation He admonished, "Pray always lest that wicked one have power in you, and remove you out of your place." (Doctrine and Covenants 93:49.)

The Savior declared to Joseph Smith, "In nothing doth man offend God, or against none is his wrath kindled, save those who confess not his hand in all things, and obey not his commandments." (Doctrine and Covenants 59:21.)

We have this instruction from our risen Lord as He minis-tered among the Nephite people on this Western Hemi-sphere: "Ye must watch and pray always, lest ye be tempted by the devil, and ye are led away captive by him. . . . Ye must watch and pray always lest ye enter into temptation; for Satan desireth to have you, that he may sift you as wheat. Therefore ye must always pray unto the Father in my name; and what-soever ye shall ask the Father in my name, which is right, be-lieving that ye shall receive, behold it shall be given unto you." (Book of Mormon, 3 Nephi 18:15, 18-21.)

Here are five ways to improve our communication with our Heavenly Father.

1. *We should pray frequently.* We should be alone with our Heavenly Father at least two or three times each day—"morning, mid-day, and evening," as the scripture indicates. (Book of Mormon, Alma 34:21.) In addition, we are told to pray always. (Book of Mormon, 2 Nephi 32:9; Doctrine and Covenants 88:126.) This means that our hearts should be full, drawn out in prayer unto our Heavenly Father continually. (Alma 34:27.)

2. *We should find an appropriate place where we can meditate and pray.* We are admonished that this should be "in [our] closets, and [our] secret places, and in [our] wilder-ness." (Alma 34:26.) That is, it should be free from distrac-tion, in secret. (3 Nephi 13:5-6.)

3. *We should prepare ourselves for prayer.* If we do not feel like praying, then we should pray until we do feel like praying. We should be humble. (Doctrine and Covenants 112:10.) We should pray for forgiveness and mercy. (Alma 34:17-18.) We must forgive anyone against whom we have bad feelings. (Mark 11:25.) Yet the scriptures warn that our prayers will be vain if we "turn away the needy, and the naked, and visit not the sick and afflicted, and impart [not] of [our] substance." (Alma 34:28.)

4. *Our prayers should be meaningful and pertinent.* We should avoid using the same phrases in each prayer. Any of us would become offended if a friend said the same few words to us each day, treated the conversation as a chore, and could hardly wait to finish in order to turn on the television set and forget us.

In all of our prayers it is well to use the sacred pronouns of the scriptures—*thee, thou, thy,* and *thine*—when addressing Deity instead of the more common pronouns of *you, your,* and *yours.* By doing so, we show greater respect to Deity.

For what should we pray? We should pray about our work, against the power of our enemies and the devil, for our welfare and the welfare of those around us. We should counsel with the Lord regarding all our decisions and activities. (Alma 37:36-37.) We should be grateful enough to give thanks for all we have. (Doctrine and Covenants 59:21.) We should confess His hand in all things. Ingratitude is one of our great sins.

The Lord has declared in modern revelation: "And he who receiveth all things with thankfulness shall be made glorious; and the things of this earth shall be added unto him, even an hundred fold, yea, more." (Doctrine and Covenants 78:19.)

We should ask for what we need, taking care that we not

ask for things that would be to our detriment. (James 4:3.) We should ask for strength to overcome our problems. (Alma 31:31-33.) We should pray for the inspiration and well-being of the president of the Church, the General Authorities, our stake president, our bishop, our quorum president, our home teachers, family members, and our civic leaders. Other suggestions could be made, but with the help of the Holy Ghost we will know about what we should pray. (Romans 8:26-27.)

5. *After making a request through prayer, we have a responsibility to assist in its being granted.* We should listen. Perhaps while we are on our knees, the Lord wants to counsel us.

President David O. McKay taught: "Sincere praying implies that when we ask for any virtue or blessing, we should work for the blessing and cultivate the virtue."

All through my life the counsel to depend on prayer has been prized above almost any other advice I have ever received. It has become an integral part of me—an anchor, a constant source of strength, and the basis of my knowledge of things divine.

"Remember that whatever you do or wherever you are, you are never alone," was my father's familiar counsel. Our Heavenly Father is always near. We can reach out and receive His aid through prayer. I have found this counsel to be true. Thank God we can reach out and tap that unseen power, without which no man can do his best.

When I was a young missionary in northern England in 1922, opposition to the Church became very intense. It became so strong that at one time the mission president asked that we discontinue all street meetings, and in some places tracting also was discontinued.

My companion and I were invited to travel to South Shields and speak in sacrament meeting. The invitation said,

"We feel sure we can fill the little chapel. Many of the people over here do not believe the falsehoods printed about us. If you'll come, we're sure that we'll have a great meeting."

We accepted this invitation and fasted and prayed sincerely about what to say. My companion had planned to talk on the first principles of the gospel. I had studied hard in preparation for a talk on the apostasy.

When we arrived, we found a wonderful spirit in the meeting. My companion spoke first and gave an inspirational message. I then responded, talking with a freedom I had never before experienced in my life. When I sat down, I realized that I had not even mentioned the apostasy. Instead I had talked about the Prophet Joseph Smith and borne my witness of his divine mission and to the truthfulness of the Book of Mormon.

After the meeting, several nonmembers came forward and said, "Tonight we received a witness that Mormonism is true. We are now ready for baptism."

This was an answer to our fasting and prayers, for we prayed to say only that which would touch the hearts of the investigators.

In 1946 I was assigned by President George Albert Smith to go to war-torn Europe to reestablish our missions from Norway to South Africa and to set up a program for the distribution of welfare supplies—food, clothing, bedding, and so forth.

We established headquarters in London and then made preliminary arrangements with the military on the continent. One of the first men I wished to see was the commander of the American forces in Europe. He was stationed in Frankfurt, Germany.

When we arrived in Frankfurt, my companion and I went to seek an appointment with the general. But we were told by the appointment officer, "Gentlemen, there will be no opportunity for you to see the general for at least three days. He's very busy, and his schedule is filled up with appointments."

I said, "It is very important that we see him, and we can't wait that long. We are due in Berlin tomorrow."

He said, "I'm sorry."

We left the building, went out to our car, removed our hats, and united in prayer. Then we went back into the building and found a different officer at the appointment post. In less than fifteen minutes we were in the presence of the general.

We had prayed that we would be able to see him and to touch his heart, knowing that all relief supplies contributed from any source were required to be placed into the hands of the military for distribution. Our objective, as we explained to the general, was to distribute our own supplies to our own people, through our own channels, and also to make gifts for general feeding of children. We explained the Church welfare program and how it operated.

Finally he said, "Gentlemen, you go ahead and collect your supplies, and by the time you get them collected, the policy may be changed."

We replied, "General, our supplies are already collected. They are always collected. Within twenty-four hours from the time I wire the First Presidency of the Church in Salt Lake City, carloads of supplies will be rolling toward Germany. We have many storehouses filled with basic commodities."

He then admitted, "I've never heard of a people with such vision." His heart was touched as we had prayed it would be. Before we left his office, we had written authorization to make our own distribution to our own people through our own channels.

It is soul-satisfying to know that God is mindful of us and ready to respond when we place our trust in Him and do that which is right. There is no place for fear among men and women who place their trust in the Almighty and who do not hesitate to humble themselves in seeking divine guidance through prayer. Though persecutions arise, though reverses come, in prayer we can find reassurance, for God will speak peace to the soul. That peace, that spirit of serenity, is life's greatest blessing.

As a boy in the Aaronic Priesthood, I learned a poem about prayer that has remained with me to this day.

> *I know not by what methods rare*
> *But this I know, God answers prayer.*
> *I know that He has given His word,*
> *Which tells me prayer is always heard,*
> *And will be answered, soon or late.*
> *And so I pray and calmly wait.*
> *I know not if the blessing sought*
> *Will come in just the way I thought;*
> *But leave my prayers with Him alone,*
> *Whose will is wiser than my own,*
> *Assured that He will grant my quest,*
> *Or send some answer far more blessed.*
> —Eliza M. Hickok, "Prayer"

Chapter Five

Walk in His Steps

And Jesus increased in wisdom and stature, and in favour with God and man. (Luke 2:52)

The apostle Paul testified that Jesus "was in all points tempted like as we are, yet without sin." (Hebrews 4:15.) In His encounters with the adversary, He demonstrated how to overcome temptation. He thus became our great Exemplar.

Because He is our example, it is instructive to ask how He prepared Himself during those thirty years for His three-year public ministry. Turning to the book of Luke in the New Testament, we read these words: "And Jesus increased in wisdom and stature, and in favour with God and man."

We too should be moving from grace to grace in wisdom and stature and in favor with God and man. Consider four areas of Jesus' personal preparation. To walk in His steps, we also should increase in these same four areas.

Jesus Increased in Wisdom

Wisdom is the proper application of true knowledge. Not all knowledge has the same worth, nor are all truths equally valuable. The truths upon which our eternal salvation rests are the most crucial truths that we must learn. No man is truly educated unless he knows where he came from, why he is here, and where he can expect to go in the next life. He must be able to adequately answer the question Jesus posed, "What think ye of Christ?"

This world cannot teach us these things. Therefore, the most essential knowledge for us to obtain is the saving knowledge of the gospel and of its Author, even Jesus Christ.

Eternal life, the greatest gift that God can give and the life for which we all should be striving, comes from knowing our Father in heaven and His Son, Jesus Christ. As the Savior said: "This is life eternal, that they might know thee the only true God, and Jesus Christ, whom thou hast sent." (John 17:3.)

We cannot know God and Jesus without studying about them and then doing their will. This course leads to additional revealed knowledge that, if obeyed, will eventually lead us to further truths. When we follow this pattern, we will receive further light and joy, eventually leading into God's presence where we, with Him, will have a fullness.

We are admonished to seek "out of the best books words of wisdom." (Doctrine and Covenants 88:118.) Surely such books would first include the scriptures and then the words of prophets, seers, and revelators. Speaking of the president of the Church, the Lord said, "His word ye shall receive, as if from mine own mouth." (Doctrine and Covenants 21:5.)

While the gospel includes the more crucial saving truths contained within theology, it also embraces truth in other branches of learning. The Lord encouraged the early missionaries to be instructed more perfectly in "things both in heaven and in the earth, and under the earth; things which have been, things which are, things which must surely come to pass; things which are at home, things which are abroad; the wars and the perplexities of the nations, and the judgments which are on the land; and a knowledge also of countries and of kingdoms." (Doctrine and Covenants 88:79.)

With the abundance of books available today, it is a mark of a truly educated person to know what *not* to read. Of the making of books there is no end. (Ecclesiastes 12:12.) In our reading we would do well to follow the counsel of John Wesley's mother: Avoid "whatever weakens your reason, impairs the tenderness of your conscience, obscures your sense of God, takes off your relish for spiritual things, or . . . increases the authority of the body over the mind."

But wisdom is not just obtained from study nor from books. The Prophet Joseph Smith said, "The best way to obtain truth and wisdom is not to ask it from books, but to go to God in prayer, and obtain divine teaching." (*History of the Church* 4:425.)

"Wisdom is the principal thing; therefore get wisdom: and with all thy getting get understanding." (Proverbs 4:7.)

Jesus Increased in Stature

There is no question that the health of the body affects the spirit, or the Lord would never have revealed the Word of Wisdom. God has never given any temporal commandments—that which affects our bodies also affects our souls. There are at least four basic areas that make a difference in our health, in our growing in stature.

First, righteousness. Sin debilitates. It affects not only the soul but also the body. The scriptures are replete with examples of the physical power that can attend the righteous. On the other hand, unrepented sin can diffuse energy and lead to both mental and physical sickness. Disease, fevers, and unexpected deaths are some of the consequences directly related to disobedience. Jesus healed a man of a physical malady and then told him, "Sin no more, lest a worse thing come unto thee." (John 5:14.) Sir Galahad claimed that his strength was as the strength of ten because his heart was pure.

Second, food. To a great extent we are physically what we eat. Most of us are acquainted with some of the prohibitions of the Word of Wisdom, such as no tea, coffee, tobacco, or alcohol. But what needs additional emphasis is the positive aspects—the need for vegetables, fruits, and grain, particularly wheat.

Third, exercise. The body needs the rejuvenation that comes from exercise. Walking in the fresh air can be exhilarating and refreshing. Properly directed running can also have some beneficial effects. Simple sit-ups or sports activities can also be helpful.

Fourth, sleep. Adequate early rest is best. The Lord states that we should "cease to sleep longer than is needful; retire to [our] bed early, that [we] may not be weary; arise early, that [our] bodies and [our] minds may be invigorated." (Doctrine and Covenants 88:124.)

"Early to bed and early to rise" is still good counsel.

Jesus Increased in Favor with God

What increases our favor with God? One of the purposes of this life is for us to be tested to see whether we will "do all things whatsoever the Lord [our] God shall command." (Pearl of Great Price, Abraham 3:25.) In short, we are to learn the will of the Lord and do it. How did Jesus increase in favor with God? Note His words: "I seek not my own will, but the will of the Father which hath sent me." (John 5:30.) What a commendable pattern for us to follow!

The essential question of life should be the same as that posed by the apostle Paul: "Lord, what wilt thou have me to do?" (Acts 9:6.) God's will for us can be determined from three sources:

1. The scriptures, particularly the Book of Mormon, of which the Prophet Joseph Smith said, "a man would get nearer to God by abiding by its precepts, than by any other book." (*History of the Church* 4:461.)

2. Inspired words from the Lord's anointed—counsel from prophets, seers, and revelators. Local Church leaders likewise are entitled to give inspired counsel for those over whom they preside.

3. The Spirit of the Lord. The people of the world have the light of Christ to help guide them, but members of the Church are entitled to the gift of the Holy Ghost. For the Holy Ghost to be fully operative in our lives, we must keep our channels clear of sin. The clearer our channels, the easier it is for us to receive God's message. And the more of His promptings we receive and follow, the greater will be our joy. If our channels are not clear of sin, then we may think we have received inspiration on a matter when it is really promptings from the devil.

In clearing our channels and keeping them clear, I would commend the careful reading of President Spencer W. Kimball's book *The Miracle of Forgiveness* (Bookcraft, 1969).

May I suggest four practices that will increase our favor with God:

First, personal prayer, morning and night. Alma, a great Book of Mormon prophet, gave this sound advice to one of his sons: "Counsel with the Lord in all thy doings, and he will direct thee for good; yea, when thou liest down at night lie down unto the Lord, that he may watch over you in your sleep; and when thou risest in the morning let thy heart be full of thanks unto God; and if ye do these things, ye shall be lifted up at the last day." (Book of Mormon, Alma 37:37.)

Second, daily scripture reading. We live in a world where the philosophies and practices of man surround us. The only way one can keep a spiritual outlook is to invest time to determine the Lord's mind and will for us. Concerning the scriptures, Jesus Christ has said: "These words are not of men nor of man, but of me; wherefore, you shall testify they are of me and not of man; for it is my voice which speaketh them unto you; for they are given by my Spirit unto you, and by my power you can read them one to another; and save it were by my power you could not have them. Wherefore, you can testify *that you have heard my voice* and *know my words.*" (Doctrine and Covenants 18:34-36; italics added.)

Third, remembering the Sabbath day and keeping it holy. Not only has the Sabbath been made a work day; it has also become a day of amusement and recreation. We please God when we set aside one day a week to worship Him and remember His Son. For He has ordained the Sabbath as "a day appointed unto you to rest from your labors, and to pay thy devotions unto the Most High. . . . Remember that on this, the Lord's day, thou shalt offer thine oblations and thy sacraments unto the Most High." (Doctrine and Covenants 59:10, 12.)

Fourth, keeping our covenants. We go to our chapels each week to worship the Lord and renew our covenants by partaking of the sacrament. We thereby promise to take His name upon us, to always remember Him, and keep all His commandments. Our agreement to keep all the commandments is our covenant with God. Only as we do this may we deserve His blessings and merit His mercy.

If we want the favor of God, we must walk in God's way.

Jesus Increased in Favor with Man

Unselfish, willing service is a key to increasing our favor with man. Jesus provided the example by a life of service. Consider the service He rendered to others: blessing Peter's mother-in-law, restoring to life a woman's son at Nain, the raising of Lazarus from the dead, forgiving the woman taken in adultery, healing the sick, opening the eyes of the blind, and teaching His gospel to bring men salvation. He blessed others wherever he went.

Because His life epitomized service to others, He can command His disciples to "go, and do thou likewise." (Luke 10:37.) Thus He said, "Whosoever will be chief among you, let him be your servant." (Matthew 20:27.) "For whosoever will save his life shall lose it: and whosoever will lose his life for my sake shall find it." (Matthew 16:25.)

We increase in favor with our fellowmen by loving them.

To walk in the steps of Jesus is to emulate His life and to look unto Him as our source of truth and example. Each of us would do well to periodically review His teachings in the Sermon on the Mount so that we are totally familiar with His way. In that sermon, one of the greatest of all sermons, we are told to be a light to others, to control our anger, to reconcile bad feelings with others before bringing gifts to the Lord, to love our enemy, to refrain from unholy and unvirtuous practices, to not allow lust to conceive in our hearts. We are further instructed how to pray, how to fast, and how to regulate our priorities. When these teachings are applied, Jesus said, we are like the wise man who built his house on a firm, solid foundation.

We, His disciples, must follow the way of the Master. He is our guide to happiness here and eternal life hereafter. Our success in life will be determined by how closely we learn to walk in His steps.

Chapter Six

What Would Jesus Do?

Look unto me in every thought; doubt not, fear not.
(Doctrine and Covenants 6:36)

The following life-changing experience happened to President George Albert Smith when he was a boy:

As a child, thirteen years of age, I went to school at the Brigham Young Academy. . . . I cannot remember much of what was said during the year that I was there, but there is one thing that I will probably never forget. . . . Dr. [Karl G.] Maeser one day stood up and said:

"Not only will you be held accountable for the things you do, but you will be held responsible for the very thoughts you think."

Being a boy, not in the habit of controlling my thoughts very much, it was quite a puzzle to me what I was to do, and it worried me. In fact, it stuck to me just like a burr. About a week or ten days after that it suddenly came to me what he meant. I could see the philosophy of it then. All at once there came to me this interpretation of what he had said: Why of course you will be held accountable for your thoughts, because when your life is completed in mortality, it will be the sum of your thoughts. That one suggestion has been a great blessing to me all my life, and it has enabled me upon many occasions to avoid thinking improperly, because I realize that I will be, when my life's labor is complete, the product of my thoughts. (*Sharing the Gospel with Others,* Deseret Book, 1948, pp. 62-63.)

Thoughts lead to acts, acts lead to habits, habits lead to character—and our character will determine our eternal destiny.

King Benjamin understood this. In the next to last verse of his great discourse recorded in the Book of Mormon, he states: "And finally, I cannot tell you all the things whereby ye may commit sin; for there are divers ways and means, even so many that I cannot number them." Then in the last verse he counsels that we must watch ourselves and our thoughts. (Mosiah 4:29-30.)

When Christ appeared on the American continent following His resurrection, He stated: "Behold, it is written by them of old time, that thou shalt not commit adultery; but I say unto you, that whosoever looketh on a woman, to lust after her, hath committed adultery already in his heart. Behold, I give unto you a commandment, that ye suffer none of these things to enter into your heart." (Book of Mormon, 3 Nephi 12:27-29.)

"Enter into your heart"—why, of course, for as the scripture states: "As he thinketh in his heart, so is he." (Proverbs 23:7.)

So critical is it that we understand the necessity of controlling our thoughts that President Spencer W. Kimball devoted a whole chapter to it in his book *The Miracle of Forgiveness.* The chapter titled "As a Man Thinketh" is the title of a book by James Allen, which President Kimball recommended. He quoted from this book three times. One quotation states:

A man does not come to the almshouse or the jail by the tyranny of fate or circumstance, but by the pathway of groveling thoughts and base desires. Nor does a pure-minded man fall suddenly into crime by stress of mere external force; the criminal thought had long been secretly fostered in the heart, and the hour of opportunity revealed its gathered power. Circumstance does not make the man; it reveals him to himself. (Quoted in *The Miracle of Forgiveness*, Bookcraft, 1969, p. 105.)

President Kimball also quoted President David O. McKay, who said: "The thought in your mind at this moment is contributing, however infinitesimally, almost imperceptibly to the shaping of your soul, even to the lineaments of your countenance . . . even passing and idle thoughts leave their impression." (Ibid.)

The mind has been likened to a stage on which only one act at a time can be performed. From one side of the wings the Lord, who loves us, is trying to put on the stage of our minds that which will bless us. From the other side of the wings the devil, who hates us, is trying to put on the stage of our minds that which will curse us.

We are the stage managers; we are the ones who decide which thought will occupy the stage. Remember, the Lord wants us to have a fullness of joy like His, while the devil wants all men to be miserable like unto himself. We are the ones who must decide whose thoughts will prevail. We are free to choose, but we are not free to alter the consequences of those choices. We will be what we think about—what we consistently allow to occupy the stage of our minds.

Sometimes we may have difficulty driving off the stage of our minds a certain evil thought. To drive it off, Elder Boyd K. Packer suggested that we sing an inspirational song of Zion or think on its words. Elder Bruce R. McConkie has recommended that after the opening song, we might preach a sermon to ourselves.

We should not invite the devil to give us a stage presentation. Usually without our realizing it, he slips into our thoughts. Our accountability begins with how we handle the evil thought immediately after it is presented. Like Jesus, we should positively and promptly terminate the temptation. We should dismiss the evil one without further argument.

It is our privilege to store our memories with good and great thoughts and bring them out on the stage of our minds at will. When the Lord faced His three great temptations in the wilderness, He immediately rebuked the devil with appropriate scripture that He had memorized.

The Lord said, "Look unto me in every thought." (Doctrine and Covenants 6:36.) Looking unto the Lord in every thought is the only possible way we can be the manner of men and women we ought to be.

The Lord asked the question of His disciples, "What manner of men ought ye to be?" He then answered His own question by saying, "Even as I am." (Book of Mormon, 3 Nephi 27:27.) To become as He is, we must have Him constantly in our thoughts. Every time we partake of the sacrament we covenant to always remember Him. (Moroni 4:3; 5:2; Doctrine and Covenants 20:77, 79.)

If thoughts make us what we are and we are to be like Christ, then we must think Christlike thoughts.

Paul, en route to Damascus to persecute the saints, saw a light from heaven and heard the voice of the Lord. Then Paul asked a question—and the persistent asking of the same question changed his life. "Lord, what wilt thou have me to do?" (Acts 9:6.) The persistent asking of that same question can also change our lives. There is no greater question that we can ask in this world. "Lord, what wilt thou have me to do?"

In his book *Stand Ye in Holy Places,* President Harold B. Lee included a chapter entitled "Lord, What Wilt Thou Have Me Do?" He began the chapter by relating this experience:

Some time ago I heard a leader in a high Church position explain his method of endeavoring to arrive at just and equitable decisions in his council meetings. He explained that as problems would be presented, he would frequently ask himself, "As measured by the record of the Master's teaching, just what would He do in this given situation, or just how would He answer this question or solve this problem?" (Deseret Book, 1974, p. 26.)

While he doesn't mention who the man was, that man in due time became the president of the Church—President David O. McKay.

My friend Tom Anderson told the following story:

There was a little crippled boy who ran a small newsstand in a crowded railroad station. He must have been about twelve years old. Every day he would sell papers, candy, gum, and magazines to the thousands of commuters passing through the terminal.

One night two men were rushing through the crowded station to catch a train. One was fifteen or twenty yards in front of the other. It was Christmas eve. Their train was scheduled to depart in a matter of minutes.

The first man turned a corner and in his haste to get home to a Christmas cocktail party plowed right into the little crippled boy. He knocked him off his stool, and candy, newspapers, and gum were scattered everywhere. Without so much as stopping, he cursed the little fellow for being there and rushed on to catch the train that would take him to celebrate Christmas in the way he had chosen for himself.

It was only a matter of seconds before the second commuter arrived on the scene. He stopped, knelt, and gently picked up the boy. After making sure the child was unhurt, the man gathered up the scattered newspapers, sweets, and magazines. Then he took his wallet and gave the boy a five-dollar bill. "Son," he said. "I think this will take care of what was lost or soiled. Merry Christmas!"

Without waiting for a reply, the commuter now picked up his briefcase and started to hurry away. As he did, the little crippled boy cupped his hands together and called out, "Mister, Mister!"

The man stopped as the boy asked, "Are you Jesus Christ?"

By the look on his face, it was obvious the commuter was embarrassed by the question. But he smiled and said, "No, son, I am not Jesus Christ. But I am trying hard to do what He would do if He were here."

Some years ago Charles Sheldon wrote a book entitled *In His Steps.* It is perhaps one of the greatest bestsellers in American history. It tells the story of a small group of people within a Christian congregation who took a pledge. The pledge was that for an entire year they earnestly and honestly would not do anything without first asking the question "What would Jesus do?" After asking themselves that question, they were to follow Jesus exactly as they knew how, no matter what the results. The book tells what happened and how their lives were revolutionized.

One of my boyhood friends revealed the impact that the idea expressed in this book had on him. He is Marion G. Romney, now first counselor in the First Presidency of the Church.

Here is his account:

During my early teens a small book or pamphlet titled "What Would Jesus Do?" came into my hands. I do not now remember the name of the author, nor do I remember what he said. The title, however, has been in my mind ever since. The question posed epitomized the desire I had had from my childhood. Countless times as I have faced challenges and vexing decisions I have asked myself "What would Jesus do?" Fortunately, I was exposed early in life to the standard works of the Church. The elementary school I attended was a Church school. Theology was one of the subjects we were required to study daily. Books being scarce, the scriptures were used as texts. It was therefore natural for me, as I pondered the question, "What would Jesus do?" to turn to the scriptures in search of the answer. There in the Gospel as recorded by St. John, I found the clear and certain answer: Jesus would always do the will of his Father. This he himself repeatedly declared.

As he taught in the temple, the Jews "marvelled, saying, How knoweth this man letters, having never learned?

"Jesus answered them, and said, My doctrine is not mine, but his that sent me.

"He that speaketh of himself seeketh his own glory: but he that seeketh his glory that sent him, the same is true, and no unrighteousness is in him.

". . . he that sent me is true; and I speak to the world those things which I have heard of him.

". . . I do nothing of myself; but as my Father hath taught me, I speak these things.

"And he that sent me is with me: the Father hath not left me alone; for I do always those things that please him.

"I and my Father are one." (John 7:15-18; 8:26, 28-29; 10:30.)

". . . Verily, verily, I say unto you, The Son can do nothing of himself, but what he seeth the Father do: for what things soever he doeth, these also doeth the Son likewise." (John 5:19.)

Having learned that Jesus would always do the will of his Father, my next objective was to find out what Jesus would do to ascertain the will of his Father. Searching the New Testament, I discovered that one thing he did was to thoroughly familiarize himself with what his Father had declared his will to be as recorded in the Old Testament. That he did this is evidenced by the fact that in his statements as recorded in the New Testament, Jesus quoted or cited scriptures from the Old Testament more than one hundred times.

Finally, and most importantly, I learned that he communed constantly with his Father through prayer. This he did not only to learn the will of his Father but also to obtain the strength to do his Father's will. He fasted and prayed forty days and forty nights at the beginning of his ministry. (Matthew 4:2; Mark 1:13; Luke 4:2.) He prayed all night just before choosing his twelve apostles. (Luke 6:12-13.) He prayed in the Garden of Gethsemane. (Matthew 26:39.) It would seem that during his earthly ministry he never made a major decision or met a crisis without praying.

From the record of his struggle in Gethsemane—". . . Father, if thou be willing, remove this cup from me; nevertheless not my will, but thine, be done. And being in an agony he prayed more earnestly: and his sweat was as it were great drops of blood falling down to the ground" (Luke 22:42, 44)—we learn that although it was not always easy or pleasant for him to do his Father's will, he always did it.

Speaking to the Prophet Joseph 1800 years later concerning his Gethsemane ordeal, Jesus said:

"Which suffering caused myself, even God, the greatest of all, to tremble because of pain, and to bleed at every pore, and to suffer both body and spirit—and would that I might not drink the bitter cup, and shrink—

"Nevertheless, glory be to the Father, and I partook and finished my preparations unto the children of men." (D&C 19:18-19.)

Relying upon the foregoing and companion scriptures, I decided in my youth that for me the best approach to the solution of problems and the resolving of questions would be to proceed as Jesus proceeded: foster an earnest desire to do the Lord's will; familiarize myself with what the Lord has revealed on the matters involved; pray with diligence and faith for an inspired understanding of his will and the courage to do it.

By following this pattern, Jesus lived a perfect life. We cannot, of course, equal his performance. We can, however, make greater progress toward it by emulating him than in any other way.

The accomplishments of such men as Nephi and the Prophet Joseph Smith have given me courage to try. Each of those great men embarked upon this course early in life.

Near the beginning of his record, Nephi wrote:

"And it came to pass that I, Nephi, being exceedingly young, nevertheless . . . having great desires to know of the mysteries of God, wherefore, I did cry unto the Lord; and behold he did visit me, and did soften my heart that I did believe all the words which had been spoken by my father. . . ." (1 Nephi 2:16.)

His appreciation of the value of the scriptures in learning the will of the Lord is evidenced by his thoughts when the angel told him to slay Laban in order to get the brass plates.

"And now, when I, Nephi, had heard these words, I remembered the words of the Lord which he spake unto me in the wilderness, saying that: Inasmuch as thy seed shall keep my commandments, they shall prosper in the land of promise.

"Yea, and I also thought that they could not keep the commandments of the Lord according to the law of Moses, save they should have the law.

"And I also knew that the law was engraven upon the plates of brass." (1 Nephi 4:14-16.)

After he obtained the record, he searched it. (1 Nephi 5:21.)

In his fifteenth year the Prophet Joseph, to learn the Lord's will as to which church he should join, searched the scriptures. Upon reading James, first chapter, fifth verse, he prayed about it. Every Latter-day Saint knows the answer that came, as recorded in the Pearl of Great Price.

The most satisfying solutions to problems and the best answers to questions that I have been able to make in my own life, I have arrived at as follows:

1. From my youth I have searched the scriptures.

2. I have tried to honestly face the challenge or question presented with a sincere desire to solve it as Jesus would solve it.

3. I have, through diligent study and prayer, sought to weigh alternatives in light of what I knew about gospel principles.

4. I have made a decision in my own mind.

5. I have then taken the matter to the Lord, told him the problem, told him that I wanted to do what was right in his view, and asked him to give me peace of mind if I have made the right decision.

This, I think, is in harmony with the pattern Jesus set by precept and example during his ministry on the earth and with the 9th section of the Doctrine and Covenants where, through the Prophet Joseph Smith, the Lord said to Oliver Cowdery:

". . . you have not understood; you have supposed that I would give it unto you, when you took no thought save it was to ask me.

"But, behold, I say unto you, that you must study it out in your mind; then you must ask me if it be right, and if it is right I will cause that your bosom shall burn within you; therefore, you shall feel that it is right.

"But if it be not right you shall have no such feelings, but you shall have a stupor of thought. . . ." (D&C 9:7-9.)

When I feel the burning in my bosom, I conclude that I have done as Jesus would have me do under the circumstances. (Marion G. Romney, "What Would Jesus Do?" *New Era,* September 1972, pp. 4-6.)

There is no greater, more thrilling, and more soul-ennobling challenge than to try to learn of Christ and walk in His steps. He walked this earth as our Exemplar. He is our Advocate with the Father. He worked out the great atoning sacrifice so we could have a fulness of joy and be exalted in accordance with His grace and our repentance and righteousness. He did all things perfectly and commands that we be perfect even as He and His Father are perfect. (See 3 Nephi 12:48.)

"What would Jesus do?" or "What would He have me do?" are the paramount personal questions of this life. Walking in His way is the greatest achievement of life.

That man or woman is most truly successful whose life most closely parallels that of the Master.

Let us look to Him in every thought.

Think on Christ!

Chapter Seven

What Manner of Men Ought We to Be?

What manner of men ought ye to be? Verily I say unto you, even as I am. (Book of Mormon, 3 Nephi 27:27)

Members of The Church of Jesus Christ of Latter-day Saints are to emulate the character of the Savior.

And what is His character?

He has identified the cardinal virtues of His divine character in a revelation to all priesthood holders who serve in His ministry. In this revelation, which was given a year before the Church was organized, He said, "Remember faith, virtue, knowledge, temperance, patience, brotherly kindness, godliness, charity, humility, diligence." (Doctrine and Covenants 4:6.) These are the virtues we are to emulate. This is the Christlike character.

Let us discuss a few of these traits.

A priesthood holder is *virtuous*. Virtuous behavior implies that he has pure thoughts and clean actions. He will not lust in his heart, for to do so is to "deny the faith" and to lose the Spirit. (Doctrine and Covenants 42:23.)

He will not commit adultery "nor do anything like unto it." (Doctrine and Covenants 59:6.) This means fornication, homosexual behavior, self-abuse, child molestation, or any other sexual perversion.

Virtue is akin to holiness, an attribute of godliness. A priesthood holder should actively seek for things that are virtuous and lovely and not that which is debasing or sordid. Virtue will "garnish [his] thoughts unceasingly." (Doctrine and Covenants 121:45.)

Whenever a priesthood holder departs from the path of virtue in any form or expression, he loses the Spirit and comes under Satan's power. He then receives the wages of him whom he has chosen to serve. As a result, sometimes the Church must take disciplinary action, for we cannot condone nor pardon unvirtuous and unrepented actions.

All priesthood holders must be morally clean to be worthy to bear the authority of Jesus Christ.

A priesthood holder is *temperate*. This means he is restrained in his emotions and verbal expressions. He does things in moderation and is not given to overindulgence. In a word, he has self-control. He is the master of his emotions, not the other way around.

A priesthood holder who would curse his wife, abuse her with words or actions, or do the same to one of his own children is guilty of grievous sin. "Can ye be angry, and not sin?" asked the apostle Paul. (Joseph Smith Translation of the Bible, Ephesians 4:26.)

If a man does not control his temper, it is a sad admission that he is not in control of his thoughts. He then becomes a victim of his own passions and emotions, which leads him to actions that are totally unfit for civilized behavior, let alone behavior for a priesthood holder.

President David O. McKay once said: "A man who cannot control his temper is not very likely to control his passion, and no matter what his pretensions in religion, he moves in daily life very close to the animal plane." (*Improvement Era,* June 1958, p. 407.)

A priesthood holder is to be *patient.* Patience is another form of self-control. It is the ability to postpone gratification and to bridle one's passions. In his relationships with loved ones, a patient man does not engage in impetuous behavior that he will later regret. Patience is composure under stress. A patient man is understanding of others' faults.

A priesthood bearer who is patient will be tolerant of the mistakes and failings of his loved ones. Because he loves them, he will not find fault nor criticize nor blame.

A priesthood bearer is *kind.* One who is kind is sympathetic and gentle with others. He is considerate of others' feelings and courteous in his behavior. He has a helpful nature. Kindness pardons others' weaknesses and faults.

Can you see how we become more Christlike as we are more virtuous, more kind, more patient, and more in control of our emotional feelings?

The apostle Paul used some vivid expressions to illustrate that a member of the Church must be different from the world. He commended us to "put on Christ," "put off . . . the old man," and "put on the new man." (See Galatians 3:27; Ephesians 4:22, 24.)

What does that mean to us as members of the Church?

It means that we must become like Jesus Christ. We must emulate His way of life in our lives. Of necessity, we must be "born again" and put aside worldly lusts and former behavior unsuited to the Christlike character. We must seek the Holy Ghost to temper our actions.

How is this done?

As I have thought about the serious sins that some of our members have committed, I have wondered, Did they seek the Lord to help them overcome their emotional outbursts or lascivious desires? Did they rely on fasting and prayer? Did they seek a priesthood blessing? Did they ask our Heavenly Father to temper their emotions by the influence of the Holy Ghost?

Jesus said we are to "hunger and thirst after righteousness." (Book of Mormon, 3 Nephi 12:6.) To do this, we must earnestly desire a righteous and virtuous life.

I cite for you an example of a man whose life was changed to a more Christlike life after he earnestly desired such a change and sought the Lord's help.

Lamoni's father was a king who had bitter enmity toward the Nephites. A great missionary by the name of Aaron, one of the sons of Mosiah, had come to the Lamanite nation to bring them the gospel. He proceeded to the king's home and subsequently engaged him in a gospel discussion about the purpose of life. Once the king became receptive to his message, Aaron taught him about Christ, the plan of salvation, and the possibility of eternal life.

This message so impressed the king that he asked Aaron, "What shall I do that I may have this eternal life of which thou hast spoken? Yea, what shall I do that I may be born of God, having this wicked spirit rooted out of my breast, and receive his Spirit, that I may be filled with joy?"

Aaron instructed him to call upon God in faith to help him repent of all his sins. The king, anxious for his own soul, did as Aaron instructed. "O God," he prayed, "Aaron hath told me that there is a God; and if there is a God, and if thou art God, wilt thou make thyself known unto me, and *I will give away all my sins to know thee.*" (Book of Mormon, Alma 22:15-18; italics added.)

Each of us must surrender our sins if we are to really

know Christ. We do not know Him until we become like Him. There are some, like this king, who must pray until they, too, have "a wicked spirit rooted" from them so they can find the same joy.

Attaining a righteous and virtuous life is within the capability of each of us if we will earnestly seek for it. If we do not have these character traits, the Lord has told us that we should "ask, and [we] shall receive; knock, and it shall be opened unto [us]." (Doctrine and Covenants 4:7.)

The apostle Peter tells us that when we possess these traits, we are not "unfruitful in the knowledge of the Lord Jesus Christ." (2 Peter 1:8.)

To know the Savior, then, is to be like Him. God will bless us to be like His Son when we make an earnest effort.

To be like Christ should be the righteous aspiration of every member of the Church. We should act as He would act in our relationships with others.

The Lord said: "If any man will come after me, let him deny himself . . . *all ungodliness, and every worldly lust,* and keep my commandments." (Joseph Smith Translation, Matthew 16:25-26; italics added.)

He expects His disciples to follow Him by their actions.

May I comment about our relationships to our wives and our families.

Our wives are our most precious eternal helpmates, our companions. They are to be cherished and loved.

There are only two commandments in which the Lord tells us to love someone with all our heart. The first is the Great Commandment: "Thou shalt love the Lord thy God with all thy heart, and with all thy soul, and with all thy mind." (Matthew 22:37.)

The second commandment to love another with all our heart is this: "Thou shalt love thy wife with all thy heart, and shalt cleave unto her and none else." (Doctrine and Covenants 42:22.)

Only two commandments in which we are commanded to love someone else with all our hearts—the Lord, our God, and our wives!

What does it mean to love someone with all our heart? It means with all our emotional feelings and our devotion. Surely when one loves his wife with all his heart, he cannot demean her, criticize her, find fault with her, or abuse her by words, sullen behavior, or actions.

What does it mean to "cleave unto her"? It means to stay close to her, to be loyal to her, to strengthen her, to communicate with her, and to express love for her.

The same applies to our families. Our homes should be havens of peace and joy for our families. Surely no child should fear his own father, especially a priesthood father. A father's duty is to make his home a place of happiness and joy. He cannot do this when there is bickering, quarreling, contention, or unrighteous behavior.

As fathers of our homes, we have a serious responsibility to assume leadership in the home. We must create homes where the Spirit of the Lord can abide. We must always remember the statement of the Savior that "the spirit of contention is not of [Him], but is of the devil." (3 Nephi 11:29.) We must not allow the adversary to be an influence in our homes.

We must be more Christlike in our attitude and behavior than what we see in the world. We should be as charitable and considerate with our loved ones as Christ is with us. He is kind, loving, and patient with each of us. Should we not reciprocate the same love to our wives and children?

Jesus asked this question of the Nephites: "What manner of men ought ye to be?" Remember His answer to them: "Verily I say unto you, *even as I am*." (3 Nephi 27:27; italics added.)

He expects us to be like Him. He expects us to demonstrate the fruits of the Spirit in our lives: "love, joy, peace, longsuffering, gentleness, goodness, faith, meekness, temperance." (Galatians 5:22-23.)

These Christlike traits should characterize each member of the Church and should permeate every Latter-day Saint home. It can be done and must be done if we are to honorably bear His name.

Never in the history of mankind has there been a greater need for us to be united in our determination and actions to be Christlike in character. To follow Him is to emulate His character.

Let us firmly resolve to put aside any action that is foreign to the nature of Christ.

Let us resolve to apply the traits of our Lord and Savior in our own lives.

Let us have His image in our countenances. (See Alma 5:14, 19.)

Let us put on Christ!

Chapter Eight

Lead Your Children to Christ

We talk of Christ, we rejoice in Christ, we preach of Christ, we prophesy of Christ, and write according to our prophecies, that our children may know to what source they may look for a remission of their sins. (Book of Mormon, 2 Nephi 25:26)

The Lord declared in modern revelation that "power is not given unto Satan to tempt little children, until they begin to become accountable." He revealed that the period of childhood was given to children so that "great things may be required at the hand of their fathers." (Doctrine and Covenants 29:47-48.)

"That great things may be required at the hand of their fathers." What confidence the Lord has in fathers, and what a responsibility He has placed on them!

Great things *are* required of fathers today.

When I think of fathers, I think of Adam, progenitor of us

all, who faithfully taught his posterity in the ways of righteousness. I think of father Abraham, whose faith knows no peer among mortal fathers. I esteem Jacob, or Israel, with a feeling akin to reverence for his diligence and long-suffering. I honor the name of Lehi for the example he gave to his sons.

In this dispensation, I think of Joseph Smith, Sr., the first person to give credence to his prophet-son's testimony. I think of the noble example of Joseph F. Smith, sixth president of the Church and father of the tenth president.

I revere these noble men, not just because they were great prophets, but because they were great fathers who realized what the Lord required of them, and they lived up to that expectation.

Consider three particular things that the Lord requires of fathers. If fathers will do them, their homes will be blessed with peace, their names will be proudly borne by their descendants, and their association with their families will be eternal.

First, fathers should provide homes where love and the Spirit of the Lord may abide.

Children are born innocent, not evil. They are not sent to earth, however, to neutral environments. They are sent to homes that, for good or evil, influence their ideas, emotions, thoughts, and standards by which future choices will be made.

One great thing the Lord requires of each father is to provide a home where a happy, positive influence for good exists. In future years the costliness of home furnishings or the number of bathrooms will not matter much. What will matter significantly is whether our children felt love and acceptance in the home. It will greatly matter whether there was happiness and laughter, or bickering and contention.

I am convinced that before a child can be influenced for

good by his or her parents, there must be a demonstration of respect and love.

President Joseph F. Smith said:

Fathers, if you wish your children to be taught in the principles of the gospel, if you wish them to be obedient to and united with you, love them! And prove to them that you do love them by your every word or act to them. For your own sake, for the love that should exist between you and your boys—however wayward they might be, . . . when you speak or talk to them, do it not in anger; do it not harshly, in a condemning spirit. Speak to them kindly; get down and weep with them, if necessary, and get them to shed tears with you if possible. Soften their hearts; get them to feel tenderly towards you. Use no lash and no violence, but . . . approach them with reason, with persuasion and love unfeigned. (*The Liahona, Elders' Journal,* October 17, 1911, pp. 260-61.)

Many suggestions could be enumerated as to what can and should be done to make our homes places of refuge and happiness.

Once a father determines that a high priority in his life is to see that his wife and his children are happy, then he will do all in his power to bring it about. I am not just speaking of satisfying material desires, but of filling other vital needs, such as the need for appreciation, compliments, comforting, encouraging, listening, and love and affection.

> *If with pleasure you are viewing*
> *Anything your child is doing,*
> *If you like him, if you love him,*
> *Let him know.*
> *Don't withhold appreciation*
> *Until others give expression—*
> *If he wins your commendation*
> *Tell him so.*
> *More than fame and more than money*
> *Is a disposition sunny,*

And some hearty warm approval
Makes one glad.
So if you think some praise is due him,
Now's the time to give it to him;
Tie him close with loving language
From his dad.[1]

Fatherhood is a supreme opportunity in life. These words directed to fathers by President David O. McKay should be framed by every father:

When one puts businesses or pleasure, or the earning of additional income, above his home, he that moment starts on the downgrade to soul weakness. When the club becomes more attractive to any man than his home, it is time for him to confess in bitter shame that he has failed to measure up to the supreme opportunity of his life, and flunked in the final test of true manhood.

The poorest shack in which love prevails over a united family is of far greater value to God and future humanity than any other riches. In such a home God can work miracles, and will work miracles. Pure hearts in a pure home are always in whispering distance of Heaven. (*Church News,* September 7, 1968, p. 4.)

Fathers need to evaluate the spirit in their homes.

Second, fathers should teach their children principles of truth and help them to understand those principles.

In a revelation to the Prophet Joseph Smith, the Lord directed fathers to bring up their children in light and truth. He rebuked several because of their failure to do so. Each father would do well to review those principles given in Doctrine and Covenants, section 93, to Joseph Smith, Jr., Frederick G. Williams, Sidney Rigdon, and Newel K. Whitney.

In this revelation the Lord states that Satan "cometh and taketh away light and truth, through disobedience, from the children of men, and because of the tradition of their fathers." (Doctrine and Covenants 93:39.) The "tradition of

[1]Adapted from Berton Braley, "Do It Now," in *Best Loved Poems of the American People* (Garden City, N.Y.: Doubleday & Company, Inc., 1936), pp. 108-9.)

their fathers" likely refers to the bad examples and teachings of fathers.

We must remember that this world is a telestial environment. Our children grow up in this environment. They are constantly exposed to television programs and movies that depict the most seamy and perverse side of life. They are barraged with slogans and advertising designed to induce them to practices that rob them of spirituality.

Some fathers leave solely to the mother or to the school the responsibility of shaping a child's ideas and standards. Too often television and movie screens shape our children's values.

We should not assume that public schools always reinforce teachings given in the home concerning ethical and moral conduct. We have seen introduced into many school systems false ideas about the theory of man's development from lower forms of life, teachings that there are no absolute values, attempts to repudiate beliefs regarded as supernatural, permissive attitudes toward sexual freedom that give sanction to immoral behavior and "alternative life-styles," such as lesbianism, homosexuality, and other perverse practices.

Such teachings not only tend to undermine the faith and morals of our young people, but they also deny the existence of God, who gave absolute laws, and the divinity of Jesus Christ. Surely we can see the moral contradiction of some who argue for the preservation of endangered species but who also sanction the abortion of unborn humans.

There is a solution, and it is that the Lord expects great things from the fathers of Israel. Fathers must take time to find out what their children are being taught and then take steps to correct false information and teaching.

I know fathers who inquire of their children each evening to determine firsthand what their children are being taught in school and what needs to be corrected. Then, if necessary, they instruct them in what the Lord has revealed. This is application of the principles that "light and truth forsake that evil one." (Doctrine and Covenants 93:37.)

The Sunday meeting schedule has been implemented to give fathers more time on the Sabbath to teach their children. This is a golden opportunity for families to study the scriptures and for children to receive instruction from their parents. Blessed is the household that does this on a consistent basis.

What should we teach? The Lord has revealed the specific curriculum that parents should teach. Note His words: "Teach it unto your children, that all men, everywhere, must repent, or they can in nowise inherit the kingdom of God, for no unclean thing can dwell there, or dwell in his presence."

As further noted in this scripture, the fundamental doctrines consist of the doctrine of the Fall, the mission of Christ and His atonement, and the first principles and ordinances of the gospel, which include faith in Christ, repentance, baptism for a remission of sins, and the gift of the Holy Ghost as the means to a sanctified life. (Pearl of Great Price, Moses 6:57-59.)

With few exceptions, righteous sons and daughters who have attained eternal blessings are not just physically begotten by their fathers. They are spiritually regenerated by the examples and teachings of their parents.

Nephi, a Book of Mormon prophet, provided a standard for all latter-day homes by this practice: "We talk of Christ, we rejoice in Christ, we preach of Christ, we prophesy of Christ, and we write according to our prophecies, that our children may know to what source they may look for a remission of their sins." (2 Nephi 25:26.)

Great fathers lead their children to Christ.

Third, fathers should set in order their own households.

Such was the Lord's counsel to fathers in early Church history, and such is His timely counsel to us today!

Setting our homes in order is keeping the commandments of God. This brings harmony and love in the home between spouse and companion and between parents and children. It is daily family prayer. It is teaching our families to understand the gospel of Jesus Christ. It is each family member keeping the commandments of God. It is husband and wife being worthy to receive a temple recommend, all family members receiving the ordinances of exaltation, and the family being sealed together for eternity. It is being free from excessive debt, with family members paying honest tithes and offerings.

Are our homes in order?

In a revelation given to President John Taylor, the Lord directed this message to the priesthood:

I call upon the heads of families to put their houses in order according to the law of God, . . . and to purify themselves before me, and to purge out iniquity from their households. And I will bless and be with you, saith the Lord, and ye shall gather together in your holy places wherein ye assemble to call upon me, and ye shall ask for such things as are right, and I will hear your prayers, and my Spirit and power shall be with you, and my blessing shall rest upon you, upon your families, your dwellings and your households, upon your flocks and herds and fields, your orchards and vineyards, and upon all that pertains to you. (*Revelation given through President John Taylor at Salt Lake City, Utah Territory,* October 13, 1882, Church Archives, pp. 2-3.)

Yes, these times require great things from fathers, and so does the Lord. Three requirements of fathers are: to create homes where love and the Spirit of the Lord may abide, to bring up their children in light and truth, and to set their homes in order.

As I travel throughout the Church and see faithful families, I say, "Thank God for exemplary fathers and mothers." As I see faithful young people and am proud of their accomplishments, I say, "Thank God for diligent fathers and mothers."

Fatherhood is not a matter of station or wealth; it is a matter of desire, diligence, and determination to see one's family exalted in the celestial kingdom. If that prize is lost, nothing else really matters.

I know of families who have as their goal that each member of the family and posterity will arrive in their heavenly home—the celestial kingdom—with no vacant chairs. They review this objective at every family reunion and mention it frequently as they mingle together between reunions.

God bless the fathers in Israel to do well the work within the walls of their own homes. With His help they shall succeed in this, their most important responsibility.

Chapter Nine

"Feed My Sheep"

Jesus saith to Simon Peter, Simon, son of Jonas, lovest thou me? . . . He saith unto him, Yea, Lord; thou knowest that I love thee. He saith unto him, Feed my sheep. (John 21:15-16)

Most of us are familiar with the Savior's description of members of the Church and their leaders. True followers He called sheep, and priesthood leaders He called shepherds.

We remember his unforgettable example of a true shepherd's concern for His sheep: "If a man have an hundred sheep, and one of them be gone astray, doth he not leave the ninety and nine, . . . and seeketh that which is gone astray? And if it so be that he find it, . . . he rejoiceth more of that sheep, than of the ninety and nine which went not astray." (Matthew 18:12-13.)

In Jesus' time, the Palestinian shepherd was noted for his protection of his sheep. Unlike modern sheepherders, the shepherd always walked ahead of his flock. He led them. The shepherd knew each of the sheep and usually had a name for each. The sheep knew his voice and trusted him and would not follow a stranger. Thus, when called, the sheep would come to him. (See John 10:14, 17.)

At night shepherds would bring their sheep to a corral called a sheepfold. High walls surrounded the sheepfold, and thorns were placed on top of the walls to prevent wild animals and thieves from climbing over. Sometimes, however, a wild animal driven by hunger would leap over the walls into the midst of the sheep, frightening them. Such a situation separated the true shepherd—one who loved his sheep—from the hireling who worked only for pay and duty.

The true shepherd was willing to give his life for the sheep. He would go in among the sheep and fight for their welfare. The hireling, on the other hand, valued his own personal safety above the sheep and would usually flee from the danger.

Jesus used this common illustration of His day to declare that He was the Good Shepherd, the True Shepherd. Because of His love for His brothers and sisters, He would willingly and voluntarily lay down His life for them. (See John 10: 17-18.) Eventually the Good Shepherd did give His life for the sheep—for you and me—for us all.

Later, during His resurrected ministry, Jesus directed Peter, "Feed my lambs. . . . Feed my sheep. . . . Feed my sheep." (John 21:15-17.) Three times this charge was repeated to the newly designated head shepherd. Do you think that Peter recalled the parable of the good shepherd? Do you think that Peter could remember what a good shepherd was to be, what he was to do? Do you think that he ever questioned his Lord's example as being too idealistic? It must have impressed Peter deeply, for tradition has it that he also willingly gave his life for the cause.

The expressive symbolism of the Good Shepherd is not without significant parallel in the Church today. The sheep need to be led by watchful shepherds. Too many are wandering: some are being enticed away by momentary distractions, and others have become completely lost.

We realize, as in times past, that some of the sheep will rebel and are "as a wild flock which fleeth from the shepherd." (Book of Mormon, Mosiah 8:21.) But most of our problems stem from lack of loving and attentive shepherding.

With a shepherd's care, many of our new members, those newly born into the gospel, would be nurtured by gospel knowledge and new standards. Such attention would ensure that there would be no returning to old habits and old friends.

With a shepherd's loving care, many of our young people, our young lambs, would not be wandering. And if they were, the crook of the shepherd's staff, a loving arm, would retrieve them.

With a shepherd's care, many of those who are now independent of the flock can still be reclaimed. Many have married outside the Church and assumed the life-styles of their marriage partners.

There are no *new* solutions to this *old* problem. The charge Jesus gave to Peter, which He emphasized by repeating it three times, is the proven solution: "Feed my lambs. . . . Feed my sheep. . . . Feed my sheep."

The answer, then, is found in shepherding the flock. In other words, priesthood watchcare. It is real concern by a true shepherd, not just the feigned concern a hireling might show.

In discussing the concept of a true shepherd, it is recognized that the Lord has given this responsibility to priesthood holders. But our sisters also have callings of "shepherding" in their charitable and loving service that they give to one another, to youth, and to children.

Here are some questions every true shepherd should ask.

Shepherds—home teachers:

Are you watching over your families as you should?

Are you ministering to their needs?

Do you care enough about your families' welfare that you find out their interests, that you remember birthdays and special events, and that you continually pray for them?

Are you the first one to the home when the family needs assistance?

Does the head of the household call on you first?

Are you attentive to the needs of each member of the family?

When one of your assigned families moves, do you know where they have moved? Do you make an effort to obtain their new address? Do you check with neighbors, friends, and relatives?

Shepherds—stake presidents, bishops, quorum leaders:

Are you welcoming into your ranks new converts?

Do they feel your love and concern?

Are new converts invited into your homes?

Do they know what family home evening is and how to use it?

Does the family feel welcome and comfortable in your midst?

Do you ordain worthy male members to offices of the priesthood following baptism?

Do you give them meaningful Church assignments?

Shepherds—stake presidents, bishops, quorum leaders:

Do you leave the ninety and nine and search after the lost one?

Do you call and appoint advisers and others who can reach impressionable youth and visit them on their "own ground"?

Have you fully implemented the youth program, and are you using this program to meet the individual needs of each youth?

Are you watchful over the young singles, the divorced, and those with special needs?

Do you carefully and spiritually prepare those who enter military service?

Are you especially attentive to young men between the transition period from Aaronic Priesthood to Melchizedek Priesthood?

Bishops, do you make sure they come under the care of their new shepherd, the quorum president?

Do you provide significant Church-service opportunities for our returned missionaries so that these young men and women do not drift into inactivity because they do not have occasion to serve as they have been doing for eighteen months?

Do you use visiting teachers to augment home teaching?

Are you teaching fathers their duties?

Do you have temple preparation seminars to encourage prospective elders to prepare for the Melchizedek Priesthood and the temple?

Do you have older prospective elders assigned to the high priests and invited to join those with whom they would feel most comfortable?

Are younger prospective elders invited to participate with the elders quorums?

Some leaders say that some men are past hope, but, as the angel told Abraham, nothing is impossible with the Lord! One brother who was regarded by some as a hopeless case tearfully exclaimed to the temple worker at the sealing altar, "I don't know why I waited so long for this blessing!"

In a recent Saturday evening meeting of leaders I heard a determined brother state, "I've sure had a time with the devil since I started to become active. Prior to that time, I just went along with him."

Are you helping the one who needs help because he has started on the way back to full activity?

Shepherds—stake presidents, bishops, quorum leaders:

Are you attentive to the records of Church members under your charge—especially those who are not participating with you in meetings?

Do you obtain forwarding addresses from home teachers when members leave your midst, or are you just relieved to get them off your records and send their records to the "address unknown" file?

Shepherds—fathers in Israel:

Are you holding family prayer with your family, morning and evening?

Do you hold a regular, consistent, inspiring family home evening once a week?

Do you lead out in spiritual matters?

Is your example what it should be before those whom you lead?

Do you ask and pray for the welfare of your own?

Do you love them?

Would you give your life for them?

Shepherds—all who hold the priesthood:

Let us solemnly evaluate our performance in relation to these matters.

The Lord calls on us, as Paul did to the elders of Ephesus: "Take heed therefore unto yourselves, and to all the flock, over the which the Holy Ghost hath made you overseers, *to feed the church of God,* which he hath purchased with his own blood." (Acts 20:28; italics added.)

Today our Lord repeats the same charge He gave Peter. He repeats it with the same emphasis, the same repetition: "Feed my lambs. . . . Feed my sheep. . . . Feed my sheep!"

Chapter Ten

The Kingdom of God Is Among You

Behold, the kingdom of God is [among] you. (Luke 17:21)

Mormonism, as it is known to the world, has emerged as a worldwide church. The growth phenomenon alone (now over five million members) has focused attention on the Church. Indeed, one of our major challenges is to cope with growth. But generally speaking, people are not attracted to an organization or a church simply because it is growing. There must be other reasons that explain the appeal.

The Church of Jesus Christ of Latter-day Saints has a distinctive message. If our message is true—as we proclaim it is—it constitutes the most important message for mankind since the resurrection of our Lord.

Most are familiar with the fact that the major Protestant

denominations came about as a protest movement against the dominant church. A few courageous men sought to reform the church internally, but this was met with resistance. Thus the great Reformation movement was born—and with it a multiplicity of sects, each emphasizing their peculiar interpretation of the Bible.

The reformers recognized error and attempted to correct it. Martin Luther said: "I have sought nothing beyond reforming the Church in conformity with the Holy Scriptures." Also, "Christianity has ceased to exist among those who should have preserved it."

After America was discovered, many emigrated to this promised land to avoid religious persecution in their own countries. Among these was the Smith family who settled in Vermont. In 1796 Joseph Smith married Lucy Mack, whose people came from New Hampshire. They were a typical New England family who read the Bible and had prayer but, like many others, affiliated with no church. On December 23, 1805, their third son was born. He was given the name of his father—Joseph.

Western New York at this time was frontier territory. For those willing to work, clear the land, and till the virgin soil, New York offered economic opportunities. Thousands migrated there to better their lot. The Smith family arrived in 1816 and settled in the town of Palmyra, a short distance from Rochester.

The year 1820 and the year just preceding were filled with religious excitement. Ministers from various denominations came with revival camp meetings to convert the new settlers. Joseph Smith, Jr., heard their preaching but remained uncommitted to any faith. The more he listened, the more distressed he became, because each denomination professed to be right. In the midst of a contentious competition for converts, young Joseph asked, "Who of all these parties are right; or, are they all wrong together? If any one of them be right, which is it, and how shall I know it?" (Pearl of Great Price, Joseph Smith–History 1:10.)

Under these circumstances, he read one day these words in his Bible: "If any of you lack wisdom, let him ask of God, that giveth to all men liberally, and upbraideth not; and it shall be given him. But let him ask in faith, nothing wavering." (James 1:5-6.)

He later wrote: "Never did any passage of scripture come with more power to the heart of man than this did at this time to mine. . . . I reflected on it again and again. . . . I at length came to the determination to ask of God, concluding that if he gave wisdom to them that lacked wisdom, and would give liberally, and not upbraid, I might venture." (Joseph Smith–History 1:12-13.)

Joseph sought a secluded spot in a wooded area near his father's farm. Here is a description, in his own words, of what transpired:

After I had retired to the place where I had previously designed to go, having looked around me, and finding myself alone, I kneeled down and began to offer up the desires of my heart to God. I had scarcely done so, when immediately I was seized upon by some power which entirely overcame me, and had such an astonishing influence over me as to bind my tongue so that I could not speak. Thick darkness gathered around me, and it seemed to me for a time as if I were doomed to sudden destruction.

But, exerting all my powers to call upon God to deliver me out of the power of this enemy which had seized upon me, and at the very moment when I was ready to sink into despair and abandon myself to destruction—not to an imaginary ruin, but to the power of some actual being from the unseen world, who had such marvelous power as I had never before felt in any being—just at this moment of great alarm, I saw a pillar of light exactly over my head, above the brightness of the sun, which descended gradually until it fell upon me.

It no sooner appeared than I found myself delivered from the enemy which held me bound. When the light rested upon me I saw two Personages, whose brightness and glory defy all description, standing above me in the air. One of them spake unto me, calling me by name and said, pointing to the other—*This is My Beloved Son. Hear Him!* (Joseph Smith–History 1:15-17.)

Young Joseph was instructed to join none of the churches, because the Savior said their doctrines had been corrupted. He was told that a restoration of Christ's original church would follow and that he would be an instrument in His hands in effecting this restoration.

We do not look on the Reformers as being wrong—they recognized that the pure doctrine of Christ was corrupted. But a reformation was not sufficient to correct the apostasy. There had to be a restoration of authority and ordinances, and these had to come through revelation. Roger Williams, founder of the Baptist movement in America, acknowledged this truth when he said, "There is no regularly constituted church on earth, nor any person qualified to administer any church ordinances; nor can there be until new apostles are sent by the Great Head of the Church for whose coming I am seeking."

Joseph Smith was greatly surprised at the reaction of friends and acquaintances when he informed them of his communication from God. A Methodist minister said it was "of the devil." Others ridiculed him. Referring to this experience, he wrote:

I have thought since, that I felt much like Paul, when he made his defense before King Agrippa, and related the account of the vision he had when he saw a light, and heard a voice; but still there were but few who believed him; some said he was dishonest, others said he was mad; and he was ridiculed and reviled. But all this did not destroy the reality of his vision. . . .

So it was with me. I had actually seen a light, and in the midst of that light I saw two Personages, and they did in reality speak to me; and though I was hated and persecuted for saying that I had seen a vision, yet it was true; and while they were persecuting me, reviling me, and speaking all manner of evil against me falsely for so saying, I was led to say in my heart: Why persecute me for telling the truth? I have actually seen a vision; and who am I that I can withstand God, or why does the world think to make me deny what I have actually seen? For I had seen a vision; I knew it, and I knew that God knew it, and I could not deny it, neither dared I do it; at least I knew that by so doing I would offend God, and come under condemnation. (Joseph Smith–History 1:24-25.)

This message constitutes the heart and the foundation of the Church. If Joseph Smith's testimony of seeing God the Father and His Son, Jesus Christ, is not true, then Mormonism represents a false system of belief. But if this vision was reality—and there are thousands who attest that it is by the verifying witness of God's Holy Spirit—then the Church of Jesus Christ was and is restored on earth again.

What then is the unique message that the Church proclaims to others? Why is there such an effort to make others aware of this message?

The most evident truth that emerged from the Prophet's experience in 1820 was the reality of God's existence and the fact that Jesus Christ was indeed resurrected. He saw them as separate, distinct, glorified Personages who spoke to him as one man speaks to another.

The Prophet later learned that all men are literally offspring of God and that mortal life was not the beginning of our life, nor is death the end of our progress.

All men and women were spiritually created by God before they were endowed with a mortal body. We lived with Him as intelligent beings. We were given freedom of choice. What God said to Jeremiah could be said to every man, woman, and child who has come to earth: "Before I formed thee in the belly *I knew thee.*" (Jeremiah 1:5; italics added.)

Coming to earth was part of God's plan for eternal progress. Mortality was intended by God to be a short duration in which men could prove themselves to see if they would do all that the Lord commanded. While here, we receive a body, experience trial, and learn to overcome weaknesses associated with our physical bodies. We are here to learn self-mastery. By learning to govern our natures, our appetites and passions, we draw closer to the divine nature of God, thereby fulfilling the mandate of the Master to "be . . . perfect, even as [our] Father which is in heaven is perfect." (Matthew 5:48.)

But no man can come to a more godly nature by himself. Before the earth was even created, a Savior was provided to redeem all of us from Adam's fall, which is physical death and spiritual darkness.

Central to our message is the fact that Jesus Christ did come to this earth and that He experienced a unique birth. Though He had a mortal mother, He did not have a mortal father. An angel from God testified to the paternity of Jesus after Mary declared her virgin status to him: "The Holy Ghost shall come upon thee, and the power of the Highest shall overshadow thee: therefore also that holy [being] which shall be born of thee shall be called the Son of God." (Luke 1:35.)

Yes, God was the Father of Jesus' fleshly tabernacle, and Mary—a mortal woman and a virgin—was His mother. He is, therefore, the only person born who rightfully deserves the title "the Only Begotten Son of God."

Because His Father was God, Jesus Christ had power that no other human had before or since. He was God in the flesh—even the Son of God. He therefore, as scripture records, had power to do many miracles: raise the dead, cause the lame to walk and the blind to receive their sight, and cast out evil spirits.

He provided His gospel as a source of constant sustenance and nourishment to keep each individual's spirituality alive forever. His own testimony is: "Whosoever drinketh of the water that I shall give him shall never thirst; but the water that I shall give him shall be in him a well of water springing up into everlasting life." (John 4:14; italics added.)

Because He was God—even the Son of God—He could carry the weight and burden of other men's sins on Himself. Isaiah prophesied of our Savior's willingness to do this in these words: "Surely he hath borne our griefs, and carried our sorrows. . . . He was wounded for our transgressions, he was bruised for our iniquities: the chastisement of our peace was upon him; and with his stripes we are healed." (Isaiah 53:4-5.)

That holy, unselfish act of voluntarily taking upon Himself the sins of all, and doing so out of His infinite love for each of us, was accomplished in the Garden of Gethsemane and on Calvary. Through that excruciating ordeal, He took the cup and drank. He suffered the pains of all men so we would not have to suffer. He endured the humiliation and insults of His persecutors without complaint or retaliation. He bore the flogging and then the ignominy of the brutal execution—the cross.

Because He was God—even the Son of God—He alone had the power of resurrection. And so on the third day following His burial, He came forth from the tomb alive and showed Himself to many.

Because Jesus Christ lives, resurrection will come to all mankind, good and evil. But individual salvation is predicated on more than just acknowledging His atoning sacrifice. Essentially, there must be effort on the part of the individual and compliance with ordinances prescribed by God Himself.

These consist of:

1. Having total faith and commitment to Jesus Christ as the only name under heaven whereby a person may be saved.

2. Repentance, genuine remorse, and termination of past wrongdoing.

3. Baptism by immersion for the remission of sins, administered by one who has the authority of the priesthood.

4. The bestowal of the gift of the Holy Ghost by one holding the authority of the priesthood.

5. Thereafter living a life of continual righteousness and resistance to sin.

But even this is not sufficient to save a soul. No man or woman may come into the presence of God except it be by His grace and power.

Salvation consists of all men coming forward in the resurrection to graded degrees of glory, which are determined on the basis of righteous living. The Church affirms, on the basis of revelation, that there is not just *a* heaven or *a* hell to which men are assigned, but degrees of glory. As said by the apostle Paul, "There is one glory of the sun, and another glory of the moon, and another glory of the stars. . . . *So also is the resurrection of the dead.*" (1 Corinthians 15:41-42; italics added.) Salvation is thus an on-going process until one has merited God's reward.

Again I emphasize that we believe salvation does not come by mere intellectual assent to Jesus or by administration of Church sacraments. It comes only through the atoning blood of Christ, which is made effective for the individual as he subscribes to the laws and ordinances of salvation. Then, through the grace of God and by the power of the Holy Ghost, one may attain a standard of holiness to comfortably enjoy the presence of our Heavenly Father and His Son.

The ultimate joy that may be experienced beyond mortality is the continuation of family love—the love of a husband and wife and the love of parents and children. God's highest reward is reserved for those who are eternally sealed together as a family unit. We believe that "till death do you part" contracts apply only to marriages for time. But when a marriage covenant is solemnized by one who holds the keys of priesthood authority, that marriage may endure for eternity. Such marriages are solemnized in sacred edifices called temples.

In temples we also perform vicarious ordinances of salvation for those of our departed loved ones who did not have the opportunity to receive the gospel in this life. These ordinances become efficacious for those who have died when those individuals demonstrate faith in Christ, repent of their sins, and accept vicarious baptism for the remission of their sins. Thus, in our Father's mercy every soul has opportunity to accept or reject the gospel message, either in this life or in the spirit world.

Much of what I have explained comes not just from the Bible, which we fully accept as God's revealed word so far as it was correctly translated, but also through latter-day revelation. We also accept the Book of Mormon to be the word of God—a record of the ancient inhabitants of the Western Hemisphere who were privileged to have the resurrected Lord minister to them. Other revelations to Joseph Smith have been canonized in a book of revelations called the Doctrine and Covenants.

We declare that God has not left man to grope in darkness as to His mind and will. By succession and ordination, there stands on earth today a prophet of God, whom we sustain and revere as president of the Church—prophet, seer, and revelator—the same as Moses of ancient days.

This is our message. It is intended for all mankind. The Church proclaims that God spoke in times past through His prophets, has spoken again in this dispensation, and speaks now through His appointed servants.

We announce that the kingdom of God is among us. The kingdom of heaven is coming shortly, preceded by the glorious second coming of our Lord. For this most glorious event we are attempting to prepare all mankind.

In a revelation through Joseph Smith, in the early days of the restored Church, the Savior addressed all of His children both in and out of the Church and said this:

Hearken, O ye people of my church, saith the voice of him who dwells on high, and whose eyes are upon all men; yea, verily I say: Hearken ye people from afar; and ye that are upon the islands of the sea, listen together. . . .

The voice of warning shall be unto all people, by the mouths of my disciples, whom I have chosen in these last days.

And they shall go forth and none shall stay them, for I the Lord have commanded them.

Behold, this is mine authority, and the authority of my servants, and my preface unto the book of my commandments, which I have given them to publish unto you, O inhabitants of the earth. . . .

Wherefore, I the Lord, knowing the calamity which should come upon the inhabitants of the earth, called upon my servant Joseph Smith, Jun., and spake unto him from heaven, and gave him commandments;

And also gave commandments to others, that they should proclaim these things unto the world. . . .

And also those to whom these commandments were given, might have power to lay the foundation of this church, and to bring it forth out of obscurity and out of darkness, the only true and living church upon the face of the whole earth, with which I, the Lord, am well pleased, speaking unto the church collectively, and not individually. (Doctrine and Covenants 1:4-6, 17-18, 30.)

These are the words of Jesus Christ to His prophet and to all the world. This is why we are under obligation to see that this message is brought to men everywhere and why we declare it to be the most important message in the world.

Chapter Eleven

The Miracle of
the Mustard Seed

Another parable put he forth unto them, saying, The kingdom of heaven is likened unto a grain of mustard seed, which a man took, and sowed in his field: Which indeed is the least of all seeds: but when it is grown, it is the greatest among herbs, and becometh a tree, so that the birds of the air come and lodge in the branches thereof. (Matthew 13:31-32)

That the Church of Jesus Christ would have an inconspicuous beginning and then enjoy phenomenal growth was predicted. Jesus used the comparison of the small mustard seed to describe the early beginning of His church. But eventually, He declared, that insignificant seed would become a great tree, and many would find refuge in its branches.

April 6, 1830, in the state of New York, The Church of Jesus Christ of Latter-day Saints had its beginning in this dispensation, a beginning that went largely unnoticed by the world. A small number of men and women, including the Prophet Joseph Smith, gathered at the home of Peter Whitmer, Sr., to witness and participate in the official organization of the Church. Today there are over five million members of the Church in seventy-two countries.

The prophet Daniel described the beginning and remarkable growth of the Church as a small stone that would become a great mountain and fill the entire earth. (See Daniel 2:34-35.)

As men have attempted to assess the Church at a given period of time, in many instances they have not been able to see its forward movement and potential. The growth of the Church, like the growth of grass or trees, has been almost imperceptible to the eye, but little by little, line by line, precept by precept, the Church has matured.

Simultaneous with the early development of the Church was a spirit of opposition and persecution. Wherever the tiny "mustard seed" was planted, attempts were made to frustrate its growth. But notwithstanding all the efforts to destroy the work—even the murder of the Prophet Joseph Smith and his brother—the Church prospered and grew. There were those who thought the Church would fail with the deaths of the martyrs, Joseph and Hyrum, but they did not perceive, as Daniel foretold, that this latter-day kingdom should "never be destroyed." (Daniel 2:44.)

Just before the Prophet's death, Brigham Young said, "The kingdom is organized; and, although as yet no bigger than a grain of mustard seed, the little plant is in a flourishing condition." (*History of the Church* 6:354.)

The Church of Jesus Christ of Latter-day Saints is, as Daniel prophesied, a spiritual kingdom "cut out of the mountain without hands," meaning that it was begun through the intervention of God. It is not just another human institution. What other organizations or churches ascribe their founding to the declaration that messengers have come from the God of heaven with authority and power to restore ordinances and keys lost by apostasy?

The Church has survived exile from four states, the harassment and persecution of its members, an extermination order from a governor, the execution of its prophet, disenfranchisement by the government, and continuous persecution of its leaders and people. That is what this church endured and survived in the first sixty years of its history— and it was through such adversity, persecution, and impoverishment that the Church gained strength and matured. By the time Joseph F. Smith, the son of the Prophet's brother Hyrum, became president of the Church, he could say, "We have passed through the stages of infancy, . . . and are indeed approaching manhood and womanhood." (*Conference Report,* April 1909, p. 2.)

Opposition to the Church did not subside with the twentieth century, but gradually people came to see us for what we stood for, rather than what our enemies said about us. Our Mormon boys fought in two world wars and were recognized for their standards and principles. During the Great Depression of the 1930s, the Church came to be known for independence, self-reliance, and care of its own. During this century, Latter-day Saints distinguished themselves in the fields of science, education, medicine, business, and other endeavors.

The missionary force brought a harvest of converts from all over the world. Seeds planted abroad as missions became stakes. Truly Zion had put on her beautiful garments; her borders had become enlarged. When Joseph Fielding Smith, son of President Joseph F. Smith, became president of the

Church, he declared: "We are coming of age as a Church and as a people. We have attained the stature and strength that is enabling us to fulfill the commission given us by God through the Prophet Joseph Smith that we should carry the glad tidings of the restoration to every nation and to all people." (*British Area Conference Report,* August 27, 1971, p. 5.)

Two years later President Smith's successor, President Harold B. Lee, said: "Today we are witnessing the demonstration of the Lord's hand even in the midst of his saints, the members of the Church. Never in this dispensation, and perhaps never before in any single period, has there been such a feeling of urgency among members of this church as today. Her boundaries are being enlarged, her stakes are being strengthened. . . . No longer might this Church be thought of as the 'Utah Church,' or as an 'American church,' but the membership of the Church is now distributed over the earth." (*Conference Report,* April 1973.)

Then President Spencer W. Kimball later added: "Since we last met, . . . we have witnessed much growth and expansion of the Lord's kingdom. . . .

"We have established new missions covering almost all of the free world, and we are turning our attention more diligently now to one day sharing the gospel with our Father's children behind the so-called iron and bamboo curtains. We have need to prepare for that day. The urgency of that preparation weighs heavily upon us. That day may come with more swiftness than we realize.

"Every year now we are adding approximately a hundred new stakes. . . . I rejoice with you, my brothers and sisters, in these statistical evidences of the progress and growth throughout Zion." (*Conference Report,* April 1979, pp. 3-4.)

As we look back on the progress of the Church, we can rejoice that the progress has been marvelous and wonderful.

We can thank the Lord for His merciful blessings. We must not hesitate to ascribe the success and progress of the Church to His omnipotent direction.

But now what of the future?

We assuredly expect additional progress, growth, and increased spirituality. We will see our missionaries cover the earth with the message of the restoration. We will see temples in every land where the gospel has penetrated, symbolizing the truth that families, living and deceased, may be joined together in love and eternal family associations. But we must also be reminded that there will be ever-present efforts to obstruct the work.

In 1845 the Quorum of the Twelve issued an epistle to the heads of state in the world. I quote from one paragraph: "As this work progresses in its onward course, and becomes more and more an object of political and religious interest and excitement, no king, ruler, or subject, no community or individual, will stand *neutral*. All will at length be influenced by one spirit or the other; and will take sides either for or against the kingdom of God." (James R. Clark, ed., *Messages of the First Presidency,* Bookcraft, 1965, 1:257.)

That day is now here. Opposition has been and will be the lot of the Saints of the kingdom in any age. The finger of scorn has been pointed at us in the past, and we may expect it in the future. We expect to see men in high places defend the Church; there will also be "pharaohs" who know neither Joseph nor his brethren. The seed, planted and watered in 1830, has now matured to a fully grown tree for all to see. Some will seek the refuge of its shade in the heat of the day, but none will be neutral in their appraisal of its fruit.

The Church will continue its opposition to error, falsehood, and immorality. The mission of the Church is to herald the message of salvation and make unmistakably clear the pathway to exaltation. Our mission is to prepare a people for the coming of the Lord. As the world drifts farther away from God and standards of virtue and honor, we may expect opposition to the work of the Church. We may expect to see the time, as the Book of Mormon forecasts, when "multitudes . . . among all the nations of the Gentiles, [gather] to fight the Lamb of God." (1 Nephi 14:13.) The power of God and the righteousness of the Saints will be the means by which the Church is spared.

Never before in our history has there been greater need for faithfulness among our members. Now is the time for all who claim membership in The Church of Jesus Christ of Latter-day Saints to stand firm and demonstrate their allegiance to the kingdom of God. It cannot be done as a critic or as an idle spectator on the sidelines. This is the time to answer the rally cry of our fathers:

> *Who's on the Lord's side? Who?*
> *Now is the time to show;*
> *We ask it fearlessly;*
> *Who's on the Lord's side? Who?*
> —*Hymns,* no. 175

Let us make President John Taylor's slogan our commitment: "The Kingdom of God or nothing!"

President Heber J. Grant and his counselors in the First Presidency gave this counsel to the Saints on the anniversary of the one-hundredth birthday of the Church:

Refrain from evil; do that which is good. Visit the sick, comfort those who are in sorrow, clothe the naked, feed the hungry, care for the widow and the fatherless. Observe the laws of health which the Lord has revealed, and keep yourselves unspotted from the sins of the world. Pay your tithes and offerings, and the Lord will open the windows of heaven and pour out blessings until there shall not be room to contain them. Be obedient to the laws of God and the civil laws of the country in which you reside, and uphold' and honor those who are chosen to administer them. (*Improvement Era,* May 1930, p. 458.)

This is timeless counsel for the Saints of God in any age.

This is the spiritual kingdom of God moving forward in its divine course to fill the earth, a truly marvelous work and a wonder! As we contemplate the miracle of the mustard seed, let us remember the prophecy of Joseph Smith, words that I testify are true:

"No unhallowed hand can stop the work from progressing; persecutions may rage, mobs may combine, armies may assemble, calumny may defame, but the truth of God will go forth boldly, nobly, and independent, till it has penetrated every continent, visited every clime, swept every country, and sounded in every ear, till the purposes of God shall be accomplished, and the Great Jehovah shall say the work is done." (*History of the Church* 4:540.)

Chapter Twelve

Preach the Gospel
to Every Nation

Go ye into all the world, and preach the gospel to every creature. (Mark 16:15)

I recall very vividly how the spirit of missionary work came into my life. I was about thirteen years of age when my father received a call to go on a mission. It was during an epidemic in the Whitney community. Parents were encouraged to go to sacrament meeting, but the children were to remain home.

Father and Mother went to sacrament meeting in a one-horse buggy. At the close of the meeting, the storekeeper opened the store just long enough for the farmers to get their mail, since the post office was in the store. There were no purchases, but in this way the farmers saved a trip to the post office on Monday.

As Father drove the horse homeward, mother opened

the mail and, to their surprise, there was a letter from Box B—a call to go on a mission. No one asked if one were ready, willing, or able. The bishop was supposed to know, and the bishop was Grandfather George T. Benson, my father's father.

As Father and Mother drove into the yard, they were both crying—something we had never seen in our family. We gathered around the buggy—there were seven of us then—and asked them what was the matter.

They said, "Everything's fine."

"Why are you crying then?" we asked.

"Come into the living room and we'll explain."

We gathered around the old sofa in the living room and Father told us what had happened. Then Mother said, "We're proud to know that Father's considered worthy to go on a mission. We're crying a bit because it means two years of separation. You know, your father and I have never been separated more than two nights at a time since our marriage—and that was when Father has gone into the canyon to get logs, posts, and firewood."

Father went on his mission, leaving Mother at home with seven children. (The eighth was born four months after he arrived in the field.) There came into that home, however, a spirit of missionary work that never left it. It was not without some sacrifice. Father had to sell our old dry farm in order to finance his mission. He had to move a married couple into part of our home to take care of the row crops, and he left his sons and wife the responsibility for the hay land, the pasture land, and a small herd of dairy cows.

Father's letters were indeed a blessing to the family. To us children, they seemed to come from halfway around the world, but they were only from Springfield and Chicago, Illinois, and Cedar Rapids and Marshalltown, Iowa. Yes, there came into our home, as a result of Father's mission, a spirit of missionary work that never left it.

Later the family grew to eleven children, seven sons and four daughters. All seven sons filled missions, some of them two or three missions. Later one daughter and her husband filled a two-year mission in Great Britain. Two sisters, both widows—one the mother of eight and the other the mother of ten—served as missionary companions in Birmingham, England. The last of the daughters and her husband recently served a mission in San Diego, California.

No other church, to my knowledge, places such an emphasis on missionary work as does The Church of Jesus Christ of Latter-day Saints. Every worthy young man is expected to serve a mission. Older couples, after their children are reared and when health and resources permit, may serve missions. But additionally, every member of the Church is expected to be a missionary by example and invitation to others to investigate our message.

A Member's Responsibility to Share the Gospel

Early in this dispensation the Savior placed on the Church the responsibility to share the gospel. On November 1, 1831, He said: "The voice of warning shall be unto all people, by the mouths of my disciples, whom I have chosen in these last days. And they shall go forth and none shall stay them, for I the Lord have commanded them." (Doctrine and Covenants 1:4-5.)

Again, on December 27, 1832, He commanded: "Behold, I sent you out to testify and warn the people, and it becometh every man who hath been warned to warn his neighbor. Therefore, they are left without excuse, and their sins are upon their own heads." (Doctrine and Covenants 88:81-82.)

When the Saints came West, President Brigham Young declared: "We wish the brethren to understand the facts just as they are; that is, there is neither man or woman in this Church who is not on a mission. That mission will last as long as they live, and it is to do good, to promote righteousness, to teach the principles of truth, and to prevail upon themselves and everybody around them to live those principles that they may obtain eternal life. This is the mission of every Latter-day Saint." (*Journal of Discourses* 12:19.)

In our day President David O. McKay pronounced a mandate that has become proverbial among the Saints—our watchword as far as missionary work is concerned:

Every member is a missionary. He or she has the responsibility of bringing somebody: a mother, a father, a neighbor, a fellow worker, an associate, somebody in touch with the messengers of the gospel. If every member will carry that responsibility, and if the arrangement to have that mother, or that father, or somebody meet the authorized representatives of the Church, no power on earth can stop this Church from growing. And personal contact is what will influence those investigators. That personal contact, the nature of it, its effect depends upon you. And that's one thing which I wish to emphasize. There's one responsibility which no man can evade, and that's the responsibility of personal influence. What you are thunders so loud in my ears, I cannot hear what you say. And what you are is the result of a silent, subtle radiation of your personality. The effect of your words and acts is tremendous in this world. Every moment of life you are changing, to a degree, the life of the whole world. (Address to the North British Mission, 1961.)

More recently, we have received this counsel from President Spencer W. Kimball:

We are still just scratching the surface of the needs of our Father's other children who dwell upon the earth. Many still hunger and thirst after truth and are kept from it only "because they know not where to find it." (Doctrine and Covenants 123:12.) There are still more places to go than there are full-time missionaries and organized missions to serve them. There are still millions more being born, living, and dying, than are hearing testimonies borne to them by the servants of the Lord.

All of this means, quite frankly, brethren, that we cannot share the gospel with every nation, kindred, tongue, and people with [our present number of] missionaries (as wonderful as they are), but we must have several million more to help them. We must, therefore, involve the members of the Church more effectively in missionary work. Member-missionary work is the key to the future growth of the Church, and it is one of the great keys to the individual growth of our members.

Leaders and members alike need in their lives the special renewal and enthusiasm which comes from regular personal involvement in missionary work. If personal missionary work is something someone has always been *meaning* to do, but has never gotten around to, then something very important and rewarding is missing in that person's life.

Good neighbors are best suited to bringing to others the good news of the gospel, just as righteous members, living the gospel by example, as well as by precept, are the Church's best advertisement. (Regional Representatives Seminar, October 3, 1980; italics added.)

These statements summarize the responsibility the Lord has laid upon us to share the gospel with all of our Father's children. We all share this great responsibility. We cannot avoid it. *Let no man or woman think that because of where we live or because of our place in society or because of our occupation or status, we are exempt from this responsibility.*

Membership in the Lord's church is a gift and a blessing that the Lord has given us in mortality, and He expects us to share that blessing with those who do not have it.

We need to live the gospel. When we live the gospel, there is a spirit that emanates from us, and good people will be attracted by that spirit. Though nothing may be said about the Church, there will be an affinity between those who have the truth and those who love truth. That is the principle of attraction to which President McKay was referring. I know it is true.

Keys to Successful Missionary Work

Missionaries sometimes ask, "How can I be successful? How does one become effective in missionary work?" Here are four proven keys to successful missionary work for both missionaries and members alike.

First, strive to obtain the Spirit.

To be successful, we must have the Spirit of the Lord. We have been taught that the Spirit will not dwell in unclean tabernacles. Therefore, one of our first priorities is to make sure our own personal lives are in order. The Lord declared, "Be ye clean that bear the vessels of the Lord." (Doctrine and Covenants 38:42.)

The Savior has given us His law about teaching His gospel: "The Spirit shall be given unto you by the prayer of faith; and if ye receive not the Spirit ye shall not teach." (Doctrine and Covenants 42:14.)

And again the Lord declared: "Seek not to declare my word, but first seek to obtain my word, and then shall your tongue be loosed; then, if you desire, you shall have my Spirit and my word, yea, the power of God unto the convincing of men." (Doctrine and Covenants 11:21.)

The sequence of steps to possessing the power of God in teaching the gospel is to first seek to obtain the word, then to understand through the Spirit, and finally to have the power to convince.

How do we obtain the Spirit? "By the prayer of faith," says the Lord. Therefore, we must pray with sincerity and real intent. We must pray for increased faith and pray for the Spirit to accompany our teaching. We should ask the Lord for forgiveness.

Our prayers must be offered in the same spirit and with the same fervor as were the prayers of Enos in the Book of Mormon. Most are familiar with that inspiring story, so I will not repeat the background. I only want to draw your attention to these words. Enos testified: "I will tell you of the wrestle which I had before God, before I received a remission of my sins." He clarified that wrestle with God. Note the fervor in his petition:

"My soul hungered."

"I kneeled down before my Maker."

"I cried unto him in mighty prayer and supplication for *mine own soul.*"

"All day long did I cry unto him."

Then Enos testified, "There came a voice unto me, saying: Enos, thy sins are forgiven thee, and thou shalt be blessed. . . . Wherefore, my guilt was swept away." When he inquired of the Lord how this had been accomplished, the Lord answered him: "Because of thy faith in Christ . . . thy faith hath *made thee whole.*" (Enos 1:2, 4-8; italics added.)

Enos was spiritually healed. Through his mighty supplications to God, he experienced what the faithful of any dispensation can experience, do experience, and must experience if they are to see God and be filled with His Spirit. We should become acquainted with Enos and the entire Book of Mormon, the greatest book in the world—a new witness for Christ.

To obtain the Spirit, we should search the scriptures daily. The Book of Mormon tells about some of the most successful missionaries who have gone forth to preach the gospel: Ammon, Aaron, Omner, and Himni—the four sons of Mosiah. They were men of God who had prepared themselves to do the work. Their example is worthy of emulation in our work. How did they prepare themselves spiritually for the work? You recall that they were converted at the same time as Alma the younger. They repented of their sins and went on a mission to the Lamanites that lasted fourteen years.

Following their most successful mission, they met their former missionary companion, the prophet Alma, quite by accident. He accounted for their success in these words: "They had waxed strong in the knowledge of the truth; for they were men of a sound understanding and they had *searched the scriptures diligently,* that they might know the word of God. But this is not all; they had given themselves to much *prayer,* and *fasting;* therefore they had the spirit of prophecy, and the spirit of revelation, and when they taught, they taught with power and authority of God." (Alma 17:2-3; italics added.)

Ammon, one of these great missionaries, testified how thousands of souls may be brought to the Lord: "Yea, he that repenteth and exerciseth faith, and bringeth forth good works, and prayeth continually without ceasing—unto such it is given to know the mysteries of God; yea, unto such it shall be given to reveal things which never have been revealed; *yea, and it shall be given unto such to bring thousands of souls to repentance,* even as it has been given unto us to bring these our brethren to repentance." (Alma 26:22; italics added.)

Note the four essential ingredients to obtaining the Spirit: the exercise of repentance, faith, good works, and prayer without ceasing as conditions to bringing souls into the Church.

Second, acquire humility.

The Lord has said that no one can assist with this work unless he is humble and full of love. (See Doctrine and Covenants 12:8.) But humility does not mean weakness. It does not mean timidity; it does not mean fear. A man can be humble and also fearless. A man can be humble and also courageous. Humility is the recognition of our dependence upon a higher power, a constant need for the Lord's support in His work.

This is King Benjamin's counsel on humility: "Humble yourselves even in the depths of humility, calling on the name of the Lord daily, and standing steadfastly in the faith of that which is to come." (Book of Mormon, Mosiah 4:11.)

To the humble, the Lord has given this promise: "If men come unto me I will show unto them their weakness. I give unto men weakness that they may be humble; and my grace is sufficient for all men that humble themselves before me; for if they humble themselves before me, and have faith in me, then will I make weak things become strong unto them." (Book of Mormon, Ether 12:27.)

It was while I was on my first mission that I discovered the constant need for dependence on the Lord. I learned through experience that I could not convince another soul to come unto Christ. I learned that one cannot convert another by just quoting scripture. Conversion comes when another is touched by the Spirit of the Lord and receives a witness, independent of the missionary, that what he or she is being taught is true.

I learned that a missionary is only a vessel through whom the Lord can transmit His Spirit. To acquire that Spirit, a missionary must humble himself in prayer and ask our Heavenly Father to use him to touch the hearts of investigators.

The first lesson of missionary work is to be dependent on the Lord for our success. We must develop an attitude that it doesn't matter where we serve, but how. We must understand that aspiring to positions of responsibility can destroy the spirit of a missionary.

I had discussed this point with a group of missionaries in Innsbruck, Austria, back in 1965, when at the end of a meeting one of the missionaries handed me this little verse:

> *"Father, where shall I work today?"*
> *And my love flowed warm and free.*
> *Then He pointed me out a tiny spot*
> *And said, "Tend that for me."*
> *I answered quickly, "Oh no, not that!*
> *Why, no one would ever see,*
> *No matter how well my work was done;*
> *Not that little place for me."*
> *And the words He spoke, they were not stern,*
> *He answered me tenderly,*

> *"Ah, little one, search that heart of thine:*
> *Art thou working for them or me?*
> *Nazareth was a little place,*
> *And so was Galilee."*

Yes, there is no true success without humility.

Third, love the people.

We must develop a love for people. Our hearts must go out to them in the pure love of the gospel, in a desire to lift them, to build them up, to point them to a higher, finer life and eventually to exaltation in the celestial kingdom of God. We emphasize the fine qualities of the people with whom we associate, and love them as children of God whom the Lord loves.

The Prophet Joseph Smith taught: "God does not look on sin with allowance, but when men have sinned, there must be allowance made for them." (*History of the Church* 5:24.) That is another way of saying God loves the sinner but condemns the sin.

We will never be effective until we learn to have sympathy for all our Father's children—until we learn to love them. People can feel when love is extended to them. Many yearn for it. When we sympathize with their feelings, they in turn will reciprocate good will to us. We will have made a friend. As the Prophet Joseph Smith taught, "Whom can I teach *but* my friends."

Fourth, work diligently.

If we want to keep the Spirit, we must work. There is no greater exhilaration or satisfaction than to know, after a hard day of work, that we have done our best.

One of the greatest secrets of missionary work is *work.* If a missionary works, he will get the Spirit; if he gets the Spirit, he will teach by the Spirit; if he teaches by the Spirit, he will touch the hearts of the people, and he will be happy. Then there will be no homesickness nor worrying about families, for all time and talents and interests are centered on the work of the ministry. Work, work, work—there is no satisfactory substitute, especially in missionary work.

We must not allow ourselves to become discouraged. Missionary work brings joy, optimism, and happiness. We must not give Satan an opportunity to discourage us. Here again, work is the answer. The Lord has given us a key by which we can overcome discouragement: "Come unto me, all ye that labour and are heavy laden, and I will give you rest. Take my yoke upon you, and learn of me; for I am meek and lowly in heart; and ye shall find rest unto your souls. For my yoke is easy, and my burden is light." (Matthew 11:28-30.)

In the Savior's time the purpose of a yoke was to get oxen pulling together in a united effort. Our Savior has a great cause to move forward. He has asked all of us to be equally yoked together to move His cause forward. It requires not only a united effort; it requires also complete dependence on Him. As He said to His early apostles, "Without me ye can do nothing." (John 15:5.)

Our work will be light and easy to bear if we will be dependent on the Lord and work.

We must not worry about being successful. We *will* be successful—there is no doubt about it. The Lord has sent us to the earth at the time of harvest. He does not expect us to fail. He has called no one to this work to fail. He expects us to succeed. The Prophet Joseph Smith said, "After all that has been said, the greatest and most important duty is to preach the Gospel." (*History of the Church* 2:478.)

We are engaged in missionary service to testify of the greatest event that has transpired in this world since the resurrection of the Master: the coming of God the Father and His Son, Jesus Christ, to the boy-prophet, Joseph Smith. We are sent out to testify of a new volume of scripture, a new witness for Christ.

Missionary work provides us the happiest years of our lives. I know whereof I speak. I have tasted the joy of missionary work. There is no work in all the world that can bring an individual greater joy and happiness. Like Ammon of old, our joy can be full because of seeing others come into the kingdom of God. Ammon declared:

"I do not boast in my own strength, nor in my own wisdom; but behold, my joy is full, yea, my heart is brim with joy, and I will rejoice in my God.

"Yea, I know that I am nothing; as to my strength I am weak; therefore I will not boast of myself, but I will boast of my God, for in his strength I can do all things." (Alma 26: 11-12.)

Chapter Thirteen

"Arise and Shine Forth"

For thus shall my church be called in the last days, even The Church of Jesus Christ of Latter-day Saints. Verily I say unto you all: Arise and shine forth, that thy light may be a standard for the nations. (Doctrine and Covenants 115:4-5)

When I came into the Twelve in 1943, there were 937,000 members of the Church. Because of World War II, the missionary program was greatly retarded. Our sacrament meeting attendance was nineteen percent. Our priesthood attendance was thirty-one percent. There were no stakes outside the United States.

We usually traveled to conferences or to the missions of the Church by train, sometimes by boat, but seldom by plane. Travel to outlying stakes would take several days at best. After World War II, the great airplane manufacturing companies were converted to civilian production, and commercial airlines came into their own. Conferences were broadcast by radio; there was no television nor sophisticated satellite communication.

Since that time some forty years ago, we have seen the Church's phenomenal growth throughout the world, particularly in South America, Central America, Mexico, and the Far East. This growth has been nothing short of miraculous.

In 1857 Wilford Woodruff prophesied that the Lamanites would rise up in strength and that "a nation [would] be born in a day." (*Journal of Discourses* 4:231.) Have we not witnessed the fulfillment of that prophecy?

Since World War II, we have seen another prophecy fulfilled. This is the return of Judah to Jerusalem—another miracle before our eyes. These occurrences have taken place within the past forty years. What marvels await our eyes in the next decade or two!

To give some idea of the recent dramatic growth of the Church, let me give you some figures:

The Church was restored and organized in 1830. It took almost one hundred years for the Church to have one hundred stakes on the earth at the same time.

The 200th stake was not formed until 1952, only twenty-four years after the first hundred came into existence.

It took eight years (1952–1960) to form the 300th stake, four years for the 400th, and six years for the 500th. The 500th stake came into existence in 1970.

Only nine years later, the 1,000th stake was organized in Nauvoo, Illinois.

During President Spencer W. Kimball's administration, the number of stakes in the Church has more than doubled.

President Kimball and I came into the Twelve in 1943 when there were only 144 stakes. We have seen over 1,200 stakes created since we became General Authorities.

Here's another interesting fact: The Church did not organize its first stake outside the United States and Canada until 1958. That was in New Zealand. Since that time, over 400 stakes have been formed outside the USA and Canada.

These figures illustrate the recent phenomenal growth of the Church, particularly since the administration of President David O. McKay. Truly The Church of Jesus Christ of Latter-day Saints today is a world church.

Nonmembers sometimes inquire, "What is a stake?" Members likewise inquire, "What is the significance of a stake? What does it mean to us as members?"

To nonmembers, a stake is similar to a diocese in other churches. A stake is a geographical area comprising a number of wards (local congregations) and presided over by a presidency.

To members, the term *stake* is a symbolic expression. Picture in your mind a great tent held up by cords extended to many stakes that are firmly secured in the ground. The prophets likened latter-day Zion to a great tent encompassing the earth. That tent was supported by cords fastened to stakes. Those stakes, of course, are various geographical organizations spread out over the earth. Presently Israel is being gathered to the various stakes of Zion.

In order to explain the purpose of a stake, let me cite a few passages of scripture. In the Doctrine and Covenants we read:

"Inasmuch as parents have children in Zion, or *in any of her stakes* which are organized, that teach them not to understand the doctrine of repentance, faith in Christ the Son of the living God, and of baptism and the gift of the Holy Ghost by the laying on of the hands, when eight years old, the sin be upon the heads of the parents. For this shall be a law unto the inhabitants of Zion, or *in any of her stakes which are organized."* (68:25-26; italics added.)

Here you see one of the major purposes of stakes. They

are organized to help parents "who have children in Zion" to teach them the gospel of Jesus Christ and administer the ordinances of salvation. Stakes are formed to perfect the Saints, and that development begins in the home with effective gospel instruction.

Only after a stake is organized may the full Church program be authorized for the benefit of the members. This means priesthood quorums for young men and adult males (high priests, seventies, and elders) and the auxiliary programs of the Church. These exist to assist the home in building and strengthening testimonies of the gospel and preparing for spiritual growth during our probation on earth.

In another revelation the Lord states: "For Zion must increase in beauty, and in holiness; her borders must be enlarged; her stakes must be strengthened; yea, verily I say unto you, Zion must arise and put on her beautiful garments." (Doctrine and Covenants 82:14.)

Here the Lord declares another great purpose of a stake: to be a beautiful emblem for all the world to see. The phrase "put on her beautiful garments" refers, of course, to the inner sanctity that must be attained by every member who calls himself or herself a Saint. Zion is "the pure in heart." (Doctrine and Covenants 97:21.)

Stakes of Zion are strengthened and Zion's borders enlarged as members reflect the standard of holiness that the Lord expects of His chosen people.

"Put on thy strength, O Zion" is an expression of prophets through the ages. This was interpreted by the Prophet Joseph Smith in this manner: "[This has] reference to those whom God should call in the last days, who should hold the power of priesthood to bring again Zion, and the redemption of Israel; and to put on her strength is to put on the authority of the priesthood, which she, Zion, has a right to by lineage." (Doctrine and Covenants 113:8.)

Yet another revelation from the Lord gives this explanation of the purpose of stakes: "Verily I say unto you all: Arise and shine forth, that thy light may be a standard for the nations; and that the gathering together upon the land of Zion, and upon her stakes, may be for a defense, and for a refuge from the storm, and from wrath when it shall be poured out without mixture upon the whole earth." (Doctrine and Covenants 115:5-6.)

In this revelation is a command to let our light so shine that it becomes a standard for the nations. A standard is a rule of measure by which one determines exactness or perfection. The Saints are to be a standard of holiness for the world to see. That is the beauty of Zion.

The Lord then reveals that the stakes of Zion are to be "for a defense, and for a refuge from the storm, and from wrath when it shall be poured out without mixture upon the whole earth." Stakes are a defense for the Saints from enemies both seen and unseen. The defense is direction provided through priesthood channels that strengthens testimony and promotes family solidarity and individual righteousness.

In His preface to His revelations in the Doctrine and Covenants, the Lord warned: "The day speedily cometh; the hour is not yet, but is nigh at hand, when peace shall be taken from the earth, and the devil shall have power over his own dominion." (1:35.)

Today, over 150 years after this revelation was given, we see the fulfillment of this prediction where Satan, in undiminished fury, is displaying power over "his own dominion"—the earth. Never has his influence been so great, and only those who have taken the Holy Spirit as their guide—and followed counsel from priesthood leaders—will be spared from the havoc of his evil influence.

The Lord also states in that prefatory revelation that He will have power over His Saints, "and shall reign in their midst." (1:36.) He does this as He works through His chosen servants and stake and ward authorities.

The Book of Mormon prophet Nephi foresaw the day when the Saints would be scattered in stakes all over the world. He saw the time when the Lord would extend His protection to them when menaced by storms of destruction that threatened their existence. Nephi prophesied: "And it came to pass that I, Nephi, beheld the power of the Lamb of God, that it descended upon the saints of the church of the Lamb, and upon the covenant people of the Lord, who were scattered upon all the face of the earth; and they were armed with righteousness and with the power of God in great glory." (Book of Mormon, 1 Nephi 14:14.)

Through revelation we know that there will be perils, calamities, and persecution in the latter days, but through righteousness the Saints may be spared. The promise of the Lord in the Book of Mormon is sure: "He will preserve the righteous by his power." (1 Nephi 22:17.)

The Purposes of Stakes

From these revelations, we can see that a stake has at least four purposes:

1. Each stake, presided over by three high priests, and supported by twelve men known as a high council, becomes a miniature church to the Saints in a specific geographic area. The purpose is to unify and perfect the members who live in those boundaries by extending to them the Church programs, ordinances, and gospel instruction.

2. Members of stakes are to be models or standards of righteousness.

3. Stakes are to be a defense. The members do this as they unify under their local priesthood officers and consecrate themselves to do their duty and keep their covenants. Those covenants, if kept, become a protection from error, evil, or calamity.

We build temples only where we have stakes. The blessings and ordinances of the temple prepare one for exaltation. Of course, it is not possible for every stake to have a temple, but we are presently witnessing some remarkable, yes, miraculous developments, in the building of temples in different parts of the world. Such a program permits members of the Church to receive the full blessings of the Lord.

4. Stakes are a refuge from the storm to be poured out over the earth.

Our Duty as Latter-day Saints

With the purposes of stakes in mind, let us summarize our duty as Latter-day Saints.

1. We must seek for opportunities to share the gospel message with others. The Savior commanded, "What manner of men ought ye to be? Verily I say unto you, even as I am." (Book of Mormon, 3 Nephi 27:27.)

2. We must seek for opportunities to share the gospel message with others. Member missionary work is the key to the future growth of the Church and one of the great keys to the individual growth of our members.

3. We should do all we can to help prepare our sons to serve missions. We should have a mission savings account for each of them.

4. Our homes should be places of refuge, love, and harmony. Under the direction of the father, we should have family prayers, gospel study, and family home evenings.

5. We should seek for the blessings and ordinances of the temple. This means that we must keep the commandments of the Lord—honesty, integrity, personal chastity, and sustaining the Lord's priesthood leadership. Male members must be worthy to be ordained to the Melchizedek Priesthood.

6. We have an obligation to do temple work for our kindred dead. This means that we must do the necessary re-

search in order for their names to be sent to the temples. We cannot be exalted without being eternally linked to our ancestors.

7. As families, we must strive to be self-reliant. Since 1936, members of the Church have been instructed to have in storage a one-year supply of food, clothing, and, where possible, fuel. This enables one to survive loss of employment, loss of income, or even calamity, as spoken of in the revelations.

8. Priesthood holders need to provide watchcare over quorum members and families through organized home teaching. They should have an interest in every fellow member of the Church to whom they may be assigned, including those who do not fully participate in Church activity.

9. We should participate in the programs and activities of the Church: keep the Sabbath as a holy day, attend our meetings, accept callings extended to us, and magnify those callings. If we give service willingly, I promise that we will have great joy.

10. Every adult member should pay a full tithe and contribute a generous fast offering.

Never has the Church had the opportunity it has today. The Church of Jesus Christ of Latter-day Saints is the most attractive religious body in the world. Its image has never been as good as it is today! We are known increasingly today for what we are and not for what our enemies have said about us.

It is possible to live in the world and not partake of the sins of the world. We are demonstrating that. That is what the Lord expects of us. This is the day when we should give it everything we have. We need to raise our sights and take advantage of the great and unprecedented opportunities that are ours as Latter-day Saints.

As we face an uncertain future in the free world, as we

face the threat of the anti-Christ and its penetration into our free countries in almost every segment of our society, people are hungry for an anchor, for something that will give them inner peace and a feeling of security. They cannot find it among the churches of the world today. They cannot find it in our uncertain economic system.

In one sense, we live in the worst of times, because sin seems to be almost everywhere and is increasing. Never has the devil been so well organized, and never has he had so many emissaries working for him. His thrust seems to be at everything that is good and uplifting and character-building. Particularly his thrust is at the home and family and at our youth. The basic principles and ideals of the past are being challenged today as never before.

On the other hand, we live in the best of times. The gospel of Jesus Christ has been restored in its fullness, together with His holy priesthood, to bless our Father's children. Our message is a world message. The Church is a world organization—the most important organization, with the greatest message in all the world.

The Lord has commanded us to arise and shine and to be a light unto the world. Let us do so as individuals so that our example will prosper the work in all the earth. Yes, let us heed the words of the great Book of Mormon prophet Moroni: "Put on thy beautiful garments, O daughter of Zion; and strengthen thy stakes and enlarge thy borders forever, that thou mayest no more be confounded, that the covenants of the Eternal Father which he hath made unto thee, O house of Israel, may be fulfilled." (Moroni 10:31.)

Chapter Fourteen

Prepare for the Great Day of the Lord

He that feareth me shall be looking forth for the great day of the Lord to come, even for the signs of the coming of the Son of Man. (Doctrine and Covenants 45:39)

During the last week of our Lord's mortal life, He was privately approached on the Mount of Olives by His disciples. They asked Him two questions, the first of which was: "Tell us when shall these things be which thou hast said concerning the destruction of the temple, and the Jews?" (Pearl of Great Price, Joseph Smith–Matthew 1:4.)

The basis for their earnest inquiry was a prophecy by Jesus that had left even the disciples stunned. While standing in the temple precincts, Jesus had declared: "There shall not be left here, upon this temple, one stone upon another that shall not be thrown down." (Joseph Smith–Matthew 1:3.)

The temple in Jerusalem was a magnificent structure. It rested on the same site as the temple of Solomon, which had been largely destroyed by Nebuchadnezzar, king of Babylon, in the siege of Jerusalem. With the help of King Cyrus the Great, whom the Lord inspired, the Jews returned from the Babylonian captivity and erected a second temple, though much inferior to Solomon's.

Later Herod the Great became the leader and undertook to reconstruct the temple. He spared no expense or labor to restore that building to the beauty and magnificence of the days of Solomon. The project took about forty-six years to complete, six years longer than the Salt Lake Temple in pioneer days. According to Josephus, a Jewish historian, some of the stones used in the foundation were prodigious in size, measuring approximately sixty feet in length. Can you imagine how improbable it must have seemed to Jesus' disciples that one stone would not be left on another? Yet, thirty-seven years later, when the Romans invaded Jerusalem, that prophecy was literally fulfilled. It is said that after Roman soldiers burned the temple, they dug up the foundation stones in the hopes of finding a treasure buried there.

The Savior also prophesied concerning the fate of the Jewish nation: "This people shall be destroyed and scattered among all nations. . . . And it shall come to pass that this generation of Jews shall not pass away until every desolation which I have told you concerning them shall come to pass." (Doctrine and Covenants 45:19, 21.)

That desolation came as predicted. In A.D. 66, the Jews rebelled against the Romans. The Roman army invaded Judea, and in one of the most bloody and horrible sieges in history, Jerusalem was eventually overcome. The siege lasted for about four years. During that time, it was estimated that over one million Jews were killed and 97,000 were taken captive and sold as slaves.

Thus, in just four decades following the crucifixion, the nation, the city, and the temple were all destroyed! As one modern historian recorded, "The destruction of the temple marked the end . . . of the Jewish state. . . . Judea was almost shorn of Jews, and those that remained lived on the edge of starvation." (Will Durant, *The Story of Civilization,* New York: Simon and Schuster, 1944, 3:545.)

Later in the first century A.D., the Jews, under the leadership of a false messiah, again attempted to recover their homeland. The Romans also crushed that rebellion; Judea was laid waste; and the remaining Jews were scattered throughout the Empire. Again the historian chronicles the literal fulfillment of Jesus' prophecy: "No other people has ever known so long an exile, or so hard a fate. . . . Scattered into every province and beyond, condemned to poverty and humiliation, unbefriended even by philosophers and saints, they retired from public affairs into private study and worship." (Ibid., 3:549.)

The prophecy of Jesus was sure and certain: "This people shall be destroyed and scattered among all nations." A lesson drawn from the Jewish catastrophe, and applicable to our times, was given by the Lord Himself in modern revelation: "My words shall not pass away; but all shall be fulfilled." (Joseph Smith–Matthew 1:35.)

The second question asked by the disciples on the Mount of Olives, and the one pertinent to our time, was: "What is the sign of thy coming, and of the end of the world, or the destruction of the wicked, which is the end of the world?" (Joseph Smith–Matthew 1:4.)

The Lord has designated these days in which we live as "the times of the Gentiles." The Gentile nations are essentially the so-called Christian nations—North and South

America and the European nations from which we came. "The times of the Gentiles" refers to that period of time extending from when the gospel was restored to the world (1830) to when the gospel will again be preached to the Jews—after the Gentiles have rejected it. This is how the Lord explained it: "When the times of the Gentiles is come in, a light shall break forth among them that sit in darkness, and it shall be the fulness of my gospel; *but they receive it not;* for they perceive not the light, and they turn their hearts from me because of the precepts of men. And in that generation shall the times of the Gentiles be fulfilled." (Doctrine and Covenants 45:28-30; italics added.)

We will know when the times of the Gentiles are approaching fulfillment by these signs:

"In that day shall be heard of wars and rumors of wars, and the whole earth shall be in commotion, and men's hearts shall fail them, and they shall say that Christ delayeth his coming until the end of the earth. And the love of men shall wax cold, and iniquity shall abound." (Doctrine and Covenants 45:26-27.)

"And again, this Gospel of the Kingdom shall be preached in all the world, for a witness unto all nations, and then shall the end come, or the destruction of the wicked." (Joseph Smith–Matthew 1:31.)

Are we not witnessing the fulfillment of these signs today? The gospel is being extended to all nations that permit our missionaries to penetrate their countries. The Church is prospering and growing. Yet in undiminished fury, and with an anxiety that his time is short (and it is), Satan, that great adversary to all men, is attempting to destroy all that we hold dear.

We constantly hear or read of wars and rumors of wars. Atheism, agnosticism, immorality, and dishonesty are flaunted in our society. Desertion, cruelty, divorce, and in-

fidelity have become commonplace, leading to a disintegra-
tion of the family. Truly we live in the times of which the
Savior spoke, when "the love of men shall wax cold, and
iniquity shall abound."

The rejection of the testimony of the servants of God
by the nations of the world will bring the consequence of
greater calamities, for the Lord Himself declared:

> After your testimony cometh the testimony of earthquakes, that
> shall cause groanings in the midst of her, and men shall fall upon
> the ground and shall not be able to stand.
>
> And also cometh the testimony of the voice of thunderings, and
> the voice of lightnings, and the voice of tempests, and the voice of
> the waves of the sea heaving themselves beyond their bounds.
>
> And all things shall be in commotion; and surely, men's hearts
> shall fail them; for fear shall come upon all people. (Doctrine and
> Covenants 88:89-91.)

> And there shall be men standing in that generation, that shall
> not pass until they shall see an overflowing scourge; for a desolat-
> ing sickness shall cover the land.
>
> But my disciples shall stand in holy places, and shall not be
> moved; but among the wicked, men shall lift up their voices and
> curse God and die.
>
> And there shall be earthquakes also in divers places, and many
> desolations; yet men will harden their hearts against me, and they
> will take up the sword, one against another, and they will kill one
> another. (Doctrine and Covenants 45:31-33.)

The world will present a scene of conflict such as has
never before been experienced. Still, men's hearts will be
hardened to the revelations from heaven. Even greater signs
shall then be given to manifest the approaching great day of
the Lord:

"And they shall see signs and wonders, for they shall be
shown forth in the heavens above, and in the earth beneath.
And they shall behold blood, and fire, and vapors of smoke.
And before the day of the Lord shall come, the sun shall be

darkened, and the moon be turned into blood, and the stars fall from heaven." (Doctrine and Covenants 45:40-42.)

I realize this is an unpleasant topic on which to dwell. I take no delight in its portrayal, nor do I look forward to the day when calamities shall come upon mankind. But these words are not my own; the Lord has spoken them. Knowing what we know as His servants, can we hesitate to raise a warning voice to all who will listen so that they may be prepared for the days ahead? Silence in the face of such calamity is sin!

But to an otherwise gloomy picture there is a bright side—the coming of our Lord in all His glory. His coming will be both glorious and terrible, depending on the spiritual condition of those who remain.

One appearance will be to the righteous saints who have gathered to the New Jerusalem here in America. In this place of refuge they will be safe from the wrath of the Lord, which will be poured out without measure on all nations. Modern revelation provides this description:

"And the glory of the Lord shall be there, and the terror of the Lord also shall be there, insomuch that the wicked will not come unto it, and it shall be called Zion. And it shall come to pass among the wicked, that every man that will not take his sword against his neighbor must needs flee unto Zion for safety. And there shall be gathered unto it out of every nation under heaven; and it shall be the only people that shall not be at war one with another." (Doctrine and Covenants 45: 67-69.)

Another appearance of the Lord will be to the Jews. To these beleaguered sons of Judah, surrounded by hostile Gentile armies, who again threaten to overrun Jerusalem, the Savior—their Messiah—will set His feet on the Mount of Olives, "and it shall cleave in twain, and the earth shall tremble, and reel to and fro, and the heavens also shall shake." (Doctrine and Covenants 45:48.)

The Lord Himself will then rout the Gentile armies, decimating their forces. (See Ezekiel 38–39.) Judah will be spared, no longer to be persecuted and scattered. The Jews will then approach their Deliverer and ask, "What are these wounds in thine hands and in thy feet?" He will say to them: "These wounds are the wounds with which I was wounded in the house of my friends. I am he who was lifted up. I am Jesus that was crucified. I am the Son of God. And then shall they weep because of their iniquities; then shall they lament because they persecuted their king." (Doctrine and Covenants 45:51-53.)

What a touching drama this will be! Jesus—Prophet, Messiah, King—will be welcomed in His own country!

Jerusalem will become an eternal city of peace. The sons of Judah will see this promise fulfilled: "After their pain, [the tribe of Judah] shall be sanctified in holiness before the Lord, to dwell in his presence day and night, forever and ever." (Doctrine and Covenants 133:35.)

Yet another appearance of Christ will be to the rest of the world. Here is His description of His coming: "The Lord shall be red in his apparel, and his garments like him that treadeth in the wine-vat. And so great shall be the glory of his presence that the sun shall hide his face in shame, and the moon shall withhold its light, and the stars shall be hurled from their places." (Doctrine and Covenants 133:48-49.)

All nations will see Him "in the clouds of heaven, clothed with power and great glory; with all the holy angels. . . . And the Lord shall utter his voice, and all the ends of the earth shall hear it; and the nations of the earth shall mourn, and they that have laughed shall see their folly. And calamity shall cover the mocker, and the scorner shall be consumed; and they that have watched for iniquity shall be hewn down and cast into the fire." (Doctrine and Covenants 45:44, 49-50.)

When the Savior spoke of these signs and prophecies to

His disciples in Jerusalem, they were apprehensive. He said to them, "Be not troubled, for, when all these things shall come to pass, ye may know that the promises which have been made unto you shall be fulfilled." (Doctrine and Covenants 45:35.)

Do we realize we are living in the days of the fulfillment of these signs and wonders? We are among those who will see many of these prophecies fulfilled. Just as certain as was the destruction of the temple at Jerusalem and the scattering of the Jews, so shall these words of the Savior be certain to our generation.

We know not the day nor the hour of His coming, but of this we may feel assured: We stand close to the great day of the Lord! In His words of modern revelation, He implores, "Seek the face of the Lord always." (Doctrine and Covenants 101:38.)

We will live in the midst of economic, political, and spiritual instability. When these signs are observed—unmistakable evidences that His coming is nigh—we need not be troubled, but "stand . . . in holy places, and be not moved, until the day of the Lord come." (Doctrine and Covenants 87:8.)

Holy men and women stand in holy places, and these holy places consist of our temples, our chapels, our homes, and the stakes of Zion, which are, as the Lord declares, "for a defense, and for a refuge from the storm, and from wrath when it shall be poured out without mixture upon the whole earth." (Doctrine and Covenants 115:6.) We must heed the Lord's counsel to the Saints of this dispensation: "Prepare yourselves for the great day of the Lord." (Doctrine and Covenants 133:10.)

This preparation must consist of more than just casual membership in the Church. We must be guided by personal revelation and the counsel of the living prophet so we will not be deceived. Our Lord has indicated who, among Church members, will stand when He appears:

"At that day, when I shall come in my glory, shall the parable be fulfilled which I spake concerning the ten virgins.

"For they that are wise and have received the truth, and *have taken the Holy Spirit for their guide,* and have not been deceived—verily I say unto you, they shall not be hewn down and cast into the fire, but shall abide the day.

"And the earth shall be given unto them for an inheritance; and they shall multiply and wax strong, and their children shall grow up without sin unto salvation.

"For the Lord shall be in their midst, and his glory shall be upon them, and he will be their king and their lawgiver." (Doctrine and Covenants 45:56-59; italics added.)

President Wilford Woodruff further prophesied in 1894: "Can you tell me where the people are who will be shielded and protected from these great calamities and judgments which are even now at our doors? I'll tell you. The priesthood of God who honor their priesthood and who are worthy of their blessings are the only ones who shall have this safety and protection. They are the only mortal beings. No other people have a right to be shielded from these judgments. They are at our doors; not even this people will escape them entirely." (*Young Women's Journal* 5 [August 1894]: 512.)

Will we be among those who are faithful to the end? Will we endure? Are we prepared? Can we live in the world and not partake of the sins of the world? Will we "arise and shine forth," as the Lord has commanded? Will we be a light and a "standard for the nations"?

Such is our challenge. Therefore, let us prepare for the great day of the Lord.

Chapter Fifteen

"Because I Live, Ye Shall Live Also"

And now, after the many testimonies which have been given of him, this is the testimony we give of him: That he lives! (Doctrine and Covenants 76:22)

There has been considerable publicity and media coverage recently on the reporting of experiences that seemingly verify that "life after life" is a reality. The ancient prophet's question asked centuries ago has been revived: "If a man die, shall he live again?" (Job 14:14.) In other words, what happens to a person once he dies? A definite answer to that question is provided by the Savior's ministry in the spirit world following His crucifixion, death, and burial.

Even before the fall of Adam, which ushered death into this world, our Heavenly Father had prepared a place for the spirits who would eventually depart this mortal life. At the time of Jesus' death, the spirit world was occupied by hosts of our Father's children who had died—from Adam's posterity to the death of Jesus—both the righteous and the wicked.

There were two grand divisions in the world of spirits. Spirits of the righteous (the just) had gone to paradise, a state of happiness, peace, and restful work. The spirits of the wicked (the unjust) had gone to prison, a state of darkness and misery. (See Book of Mormon, Alma 40:12-15.) Jesus went only to the righteous—to paradise.

Following is a portion of the glorious Vision of the Redemption of the Dead given to President Joseph F. Smith and sustained and accepted by the Church as holy scripture in April 1976:

> Gathered together in one place [was] an innumerable company of the spirits of the just, who had been faithful in the testimony of Jesus while they lived in mortality; and who had . . . suffered tribulation in their Redeemer's name. All these had departed mortal life, firm in the hope of a glorious resurrection. . . . They were filled with joy and gladness, and were rejoicing together because the day of their deliverance was at hand. They were assembled awaiting the advent of the Son of God into the spirit world, to declare their redemption from the bands of death. . . .
>
> While this vast multitude waited and conversed, rejoicing in the hour of their deliverance from the chains of death, the Son of God appeared, declaring liberty to the captives who had been faithful; and there he preached to them the everlasting gospel, the doctrine of the resurrection and the redemption of mankind from the fall, and from individual sins on conditions of repentance. . . .
>
> And the saints rejoiced in their redemption, and bowed the knee and acknowledged the Son of God as their Redeemer and Deliverer from death and the chains of hell. Their countenances shone, and the radiance from the presence of the Lord rested upon them, and they sang praises unto his holy name. (Doctrine and Covenants 138:12-16, 18-19, 23-24.)

Jesus did not go to the wicked, or to prison. They were those who were unrepentant and who "had defiled themselves while in the flesh." (Doctrine and Covenants 138:20.)

Moreover, "from among the righteous, he [the Lord] organized his forces and appointed messengers, clothed with power and authority, and commissioned them to go forth and carry the light of the gospel to them that were in darkness.... These were taught faith in God, repentance from sin, vicarious baptism for the remission of sins, the gift of the Holy Ghost by the laying on of hands, and all other principles of the gospel that were necessary for them to know in order to qualify themselves that they might be judged according to men in the flesh, but live according to God in the spirit." (Doctrine and Covenants 138:30, 33-34.)

The spirit world is not far away. From the Lord's point of view, it is all one great program on both sides of the veil. Sometimes the veil between this life and the life beyond becomes very thin. This I know! Our loved ones who have passed on are not far from us.

One Church president asked, "Where is the spirit world?" and then answered his own question: "It is right here.... Do [spirits] go beyond the boundaries of this organized earth? No, they do not. They are brought forth upon this earth, for the express purpose of inhabiting it to all eternity." He also said, "When the spirits leave their bodies they are in the presence of our Father and God; they are prepared then to see, hear and understand spiritual things.... If the Lord would permit it, and it was His will that it should be done, you could see the spirits that have departed from this world, as plainly as you now see bodies with your natural eyes." (Brigham Young, *Journal of Discourses* 3:369, 368.)

What, then, is death like? Here is a simple incident as told by my friend Dr. Peter Marshall, the late chaplain of the United States Senate:

In a home of which I know, a little boy—the only son—was ill with an incurable disease. Month after month the mother had tenderly nursed him, ... but as the weeks went on and he grew no better, the little fellow gradually began to understand . . . the meaning of the term *death* and he, too, knew that he was to die.

One day his mother had been reading to him the stirring tales of King Arthur and the Knights of the Round Table. . . . As she closed the book, the boy lay silent for an instant as though deeply stirred with the trumpet call of the old English tale, and then asked the question that had been weighing on his childish heart.

"Mother, what is it like to die? Mother, does it hurt?"

Quick tears sprang to her eyes and she fled to the kitchen supposedly to tend to something on the stove. . . . She breathed a hurried prayer that the Lord would keep her from breaking down before the boy, and would tell her what to say. And the Lord did tell her. Immediately she knew how to explain it to him.

"Kenneth," she said as she returned to the next room, "you will remember when you were a tiny boy how you used to play so hard all day that when night came you would be too tired even to undress, and you would tumble into mother's bed and fall asleep? . . . In the morning, much to your surprise, you would wake up and find yourself in your own bed in your own room. You were there because someone had loved you and taken care of you. Your father had come—with big strong arms—and carried you away.

"Kenneth, death is just like that. We just wake up some morning to find ourselves in the other room—our own room where we belong—because the Lord Jesus loves us."

The lad's shining, trusting face looking up into hers told her that the point had gone home and that there would be no more fear . . . only love and trust in his little heart as he went to meet the Father in Heaven. He never questioned again. And several weeks later he fell asleep just as she had said. That is what death is like. (Catherine Marshall, *A Man Called Peter,* New York: McGraw Hill, 1951, pp. 260-61.)

Yes, indisputably there is life after death. Mortality is a place of temporary duration—and so is the spirit world. As inevitable as death is to mortals, so also is an eventual resurrection to those in the spirit world.

On the third day following Jesus' crucifixion, there was a great earthquake. The stone was rolled back from the door of the tomb. Some of the women, among the most devoted of

His followers, came to the place with spices "and found not the body of the Lord Jesus."

Angels appeared and said simply, "Why seek ye the living among the dead? He is not here, but is risen." (Luke 24:3-6.) There is nothing in history to equal that dramatic announcement: "He is not here, but is risen."

The greatest events of history are those that affect the greatest number for the longest periods. By this standard, no event could be more important to individuals or nations than the resurrection of the Master. The eventual resurrection of every soul who has lived and died on earth is a scriptural certainty, and surely there is no event for which one should make more careful preparation. A glorious resurrection should be the goal of every man and woman, for it is a reality. Nothing is more absolutely universal than the resurrection. Every living being will be resurrected. "As in Adam all die, even so in Christ shall all be made alive." (1 Corinthians 15:22.)

Almost immediately after the glorious resurrection of the Lord, Matthew records, "the graves were opened; and many bodies of the saints which slept arose, and came out of the graves after his resurrection, and went into the holy city, and appeared unto many." (Matthew 27:52-53.)

Yes, the resurrection of Jesus Christ was a glorious reality. He became the firstfruits of them that slept. He truly rose from the tomb the third day, as He and His prophets foretold, and became in very deed "the resurrection, and the life." (John 11:25.) He broke the bands of death for all of us. We, too, will be resurrected. Our spirits will be reunited with our bodies, never to be separated.

There is abundant testimony and verification of the resurrection of Jesus Christ. Witnesses are many.

The risen Lord appeared to several women, to the two disciples on the road to Emmaus, to Peter, to the apostles, and "after that," as reported by Paul, "he was seen of above five hundred brethren at once. . . . And last of all he was seen of [Paul] also." (1 Corinthians 15:6, 8.)

Throughout the forty days following His resurrection, the Lord manifested Himself at intervals and gave instructions in things pertaining to the kingdom of God. Much that He said and did is not written, but such things as are of record, John assures us, "are written, that [we] might believe that Jesus is the Christ, the Son of God; and that believing [we] might have life through his name." (John 20:31.)

He told His followers that He must soon ascend to His Father in heaven. As the time of His ascension drew nigh, the Lord, in that last solemn interview, gave His parting instructions to His disciples.

When Christ and the disciples had gone "as far as to Bethany," where Mary, Martha, and Lazarus lived, He "lifted up his hands, and blessed them." (Luke 24:50.) And when He had spoken, He was taken up until a cloud received Him out of their sight. As the apostles stood gazing toward heaven, two personages clothed in white apparel appeared. They spoke to the eleven, saying, "Ye men of Galilee, why stand ye gazing up into heaven? this same Jesus, which is taken up from you into heaven, shall so come in like manner as ye have seen him go into heaven." (Acts 1:9-11.)

Worshipfully and with great joy, the apostles returned to Jerusalem. The Lord's ascension was accomplished. It was truly a literal departure of a material being, as His resurrection had been an actual return of His spirit to His own physical body. Now the disciples began to comprehend more fully some of His last words—"be of good cheer; I have overcome the world." (John 16:33.) Because of Christ, the grave had no permanent victory. Death was overcome!

He lives today! Of that I bear solemn witness. This same Jesus has already come to earth in our day. The resurrected

Christ—glorified, exalted, the God of this world under the Father—appeared to the boy Joseph Smith, Jr., in 1820. This same Jesus, who was the God of Abraham, Isaac, and Jacob, the God of Moses, the Creator of this earth, has come in our day. He was introduced by our Heavenly Father to Joseph Smith with these words: *"This is My Beloved Son. Hear Him!"* (Joseph Smith–History 1:17.)

There are some in our midst who sponsor the sophistry that this appearance of God the Father and His Son, Jesus Christ, was not literal, that it was probably a product of Joseph Smith's own imaginings. That is not true. This is an attempt to discredit the testimony of Joseph Smith. It is also an attempt to discredit the testimony of Jesus Himself, who came to Joseph as a witness of His own resurrection.

The appearance of God the Father and His Son, Jesus Christ, to Joseph Smith is the greatest event that has occurred in this world since the resurrection of the Master. As the restored Church of Jesus Christ, we humbly and gratefully bear this witness to all men. It is the truth, intended for all of our Father's children. Here is the further testimony of Joseph Smith and Sidney Rigdon, who received this glorious vision in February 1832:

And now, after the many testimonies which have been given of him, this is the testimony, last of all, which we give of him: That he lives!

For we saw him, even on the right hand of God; and we heard the voice bearing record that he is the Only Begotten of the Father—

That by him, and through him, and of him, the worlds are and were created, and the inhabitants thereof are begotten sons and daughters unto God. (Doctrine and Covenants 76:22-24.)

Yes, Jesus is the Christ! He broke the bands of death. He is our Savior and Redeemer, the very Son of God. And He will come again as our resurrected Lord. That day is not far distant. It is evident to all who accept the Savior's literal resurrection that life does not end at death. Our Lord promised, "Because I live, ye shall live also." (John 14:19.)

There is additional significance of His resurrection to those of us who believe and accept latter-day revelation. This is the testimony of the Prophet Joseph Smith, who described in vision how the resurrection affects the family unit:

> Would you think it strange if I relate what I have seen in vision in relation to this interesting theme [the resurrection]? Those who have died in Jesus Christ may expect to enter into all that fruition of joy when they come forth, which they possessed or anticipated here.
>
> So plain was the vision, that I actually saw men, before they ascended from the tomb, as though they were getting up slowly. They took each other by the hand and said to each other, "My father, my son, my mother, my daughter, my brother, my sister." And when the voice calls for the dead to arise, suppose I am laid by the side of my father, what would be the first joy of my heart? To meet my father, my mother, my brother, my sister; and when they are by my side, I embrace them and they me. . . .
>
> God has revealed His Son from the heavens and the doctrine of the resurrection also; and we have a knowledge that those we bury here God will bring up again, clothed upon and quickened by the Spirit of the great God; and what mattereth it whether we lay them down, or we lay down with them, when we can keep them no longer? Let these truths sink down in our hearts, that we may even here begin to enjoy that which shall be in full hereafter. (*History of the Church* 5:361-62.)

It was through Joseph Smith that the God of heaven revealed the truth that the family may endure beyond the grave—that the sympathies, affections, and love for each other may exist forever. One of the early apostles of this dispensation, Elder Parley P. Pratt, wrote:

> It was Joseph Smith who taught me how to prize the endearing relationships of father and mother, husband and wife; of brother and sister, and son and daughter.

It was from him that I learned that the wife of my bosom might be secured to me for time and all eternity; and that the refined sympathies and affections which endeared us to each other emanated from the foundation of divine eternal love. It was from him that I learned that we might cultivate these affections, and grow and increase in the same to all eternity.

It was from him that I learned the true dignity and destiny of a son of God, clothed with an eternal priesthood, as the patriarch and sovereign of his [family]. It was from him that I learned that the highest dignity of womanhood was, to stand as a queen and priestess to her husband. . . .

I had loved before, but I knew not why. But now I loved—with a pureness—an intensity of elevated, exalted feeling, which would lift my soul from the transitory things of this grovelling sphere and expand it as the ocean. I felt that God was my heavenly Father indeed; that Jesus was my brother, and that the wife of my bosom was an immortal, eternal companion, a kind of ministering angel, given to me as a comfort, and a crown of glory forever and ever. In short, I could now love with the spirit and with the understanding also. (*Autobiography of Parley P. Pratt,* Deseret Book, 1968, pp. 297-98.)

We qualify for these blessings when we go with a companion to the house of the Lord and receive the sealing ordinances that bind the family unit beyond the grave. These blessings are received in no other way, for as the Lord has decreed, "Except ye abide my law ye cannot attain to this glory" (Doctrine and Covenants 132:21), which glory is an eternal increase (see Doctrine and Covenants 132:19).

But there is another responsibility we have in binding our family units together—this, too, revealed through the Prophet of this dispensation. Jesus said to His apostles, "The works that I do shall [ye] do also; and greater works than these shall [ye] do; because I go to my Father." (John 14:12.)

One of the works He has commissioned in these latter days is that we who have received the ordinances of exaltation do the ordinance and sealing work for our progenitors who have not had the opportunity to receive the gospel while in mortality. Ours is the privilege of opening the doors of salvation to those souls who may be imprisoned in darkness in the world of spirits, that they may receive the light of the gospel and be judged the same as we. Yes, "the works I do"—proferring the saving ordinances of the gospel to others—"shall ye do also." How many thousands of our kindred yet await these sealing ordinances?

It is well to ask, "Have I done all I can as an individual on this side of the veil? Will I be a savior to them—my own progenitors?"

Without them, we cannot be made perfect! Exaltation is a family affair.

Yes, because He lives, we shall also. Because He lives, the love and family association we cherish on this side of the veil may be perpetuated into the eternities. Because He lives, we may share in the glory that is enjoyed by the holiest of all—our Father in heaven.

Chapter Sixteen

A Witness of Christ

I know that my Redeemer lives;
What comfort this sweet sentence gives!
He lives, he lives, who once was dead.
He lives, my ever-living head.

—Hymns, no. 95

I am grateful beyond measure for my personal testimony concerning the divine mission of Jesus Christ. To conclude this volume, I desire to bear witness to the divinity of Jesus Christ and to show by His deeds and honored titles given by His Father and the prophets that He is indeed deserving of our love, our reverence, and our worship.

The fundamental principle of our religion is faith in the Lord Jesus Christ. Why is it expedient to center confidence, hope, and trust in one solitary figure? Why is faith in Him so necessary to peace of mind in this life and hope in the world to come?

My answer to these questions is derived from a lifetime in His service and the confirmation of the Holy Spirit that only Jesus Christ is uniquely qualified to provide hope, confidence, and strength to overcome the world and rise above our human failings. This is the reason I place my faith and trust in Him and strive to abide by His laws and teachings.

Why faith in Jesus Christ?

Jesus Christ was and is the *Lord God Omnipotent.* (See Book of Mormon, Mosiah 3:5.) He was chosen before He was born. He was the all-powerful Creator of the heavens and the earth. He is the source of life and light to all things. His word is the law by which all things are governed in the universe. All things created and made by Him are subject to His infinite power.

Jesus Christ is the *Son of God.* He came to this earth at a foreappointed time through a royal birthright that preserved His Godhood. Combined in His nature were the human attributes of His mortal mother and the divine attributes and power of His Eternal Father.

His unique heredity made Him heir to the honored title *the Only Begotten Son of God in the flesh.* As the Son of God, He inherited powers and intelligence that no human has ever had before or since. He was literally Immanuel, which means "God with us."

Even though He was God's Son sent to earth, the divine plan of the Father required that Jesus be subjected to all the difficulties and tribulations of mortality. Thus He became subject to "temptations, . . . hunger, thirst, and fatigue." (Mosiah 3:7.)

To qualify as the *Redeemer* of all our Father's children, Jesus had to be perfectly obedient to all the laws of God. Because He subjected Himself to the will of the Father, He grew from "grace to grace, until He received a fulness" of the Father's power. Thus He had "all power, both in heaven and on earth." (Doctrine and Covenants 93:13, 17.)

Once this truth about the One we worship as the Son of God is understood, we can more readily comprehend how He had power to heal the sick, cure all manner of diseases, raise the dead, and command the elements. Even devils, whom He cast out, were subject to Him and acknowledged His divinity.

As the great *Lawgiver,* He gave laws and commandments for the benefit of all our Heavenly Father's children. Indeed, His law fulfilled all previous covenants with the house of Israel. Said He: "Behold, I am the law, and the light. Look unto me, and endure to the end, and ye shall live; for unto him that endureth to the end will I grant eternal life." (Book of Mormon, 3 Nephi 15:9.)

His law required all mankind, regardless of station in life, to repent and be baptized in His name and receive the Holy Ghost as the sanctifying power to cleanse themselves from sin. Compliance with these laws and ordinances will enable each individual to stand guiltless before Him at the day of judgment. Those who so comply are likened to one who builds his house on a firm foundation so that even "the gates of hell shall not prevail against them." (3 Nephi 11:39.)

Appropriately I praise Him as the *Rock of Our Salvation.*

To have any measure of appreciation and gratitude for what He accomplished in our behalf, these vital truths should be remembered:

Jesus came to earth to do our Father's will.

He came with a foreknowledge that He would bear the burden of the sins of us all.

He knew that He would be lifted up on the cross.

He was born to be the *Savior* and *Redeemer* of all mankind.

He was *able* to accomplish His mission because He was the Son of God and He possessed the power of God.

He was *willing* to accomplish His mission because He loves us.

No mortal being had the power or capability to redeem all other mortals from their lost and fallen condition, nor could any other voluntarily forfeit his life and thereby bring to pass a universal resurrection for all other mortals. Only Jesus Christ was able and willing to accomplish such a redeeming act of love.

We may never understand nor comprehend in mortality *how* He accomplished what He did, but we must not fail to understand *why* He did what He did.

All that He did was prompted by His unselfish, infinite love for us. Examine His own words: "For behold, I, God, have suffered these things for all, that they might not suffer if they would repent; . . . Which suffering caused myself, even God, the greatest of all, to tremble because of pain, and to bleed at every pore, and to suffer both body and spirit—and would that I might not drink the bitter cup, and shrink." (Doctrine and Covenants 19:16, 18.)

As was so characteristic of His entire mortal experience, the Savior submitted to our Father's will and took the bitter cup and drank. He suffered the pains of all men in Gethsemane so they would not have to suffer if they would repent. He submitted Himself to humiliation and insults from His enemies without complaint or retaliation. And, finally, He endured the flogging and brutal shame of the cross. Only then did He voluntarily submit to death. Again, He explained: "No man taketh [my life] from me, but I lay it down of myself. I have power to lay it down, and I have power to take it again. This commandment have I received of my Father." (John 10:18.)

He is the *Resurrection* and the *Life.* (John 11:25.) This power to revive His own life was possible because Jesus Christ was God—even the Son of God. Because He had the power to overcome death, all mankind will be resurrected. "Because I live, ye shall live also," He testified. (John 14:19.)

How I reverence His name—yes, even the hallowed titles that represent His deeds!

He is our *Great Exemplar.*

He was perfectly obedient to our Heavenly Father and showed us how to forsake the world and keep our priorities in perspective. Because of His love for us, He showed us how to rise above petty weaknesses and to demonstrate affection, love, and charity in our relationships with others.

He is the *Bread of Life.* By fasting, prayer, and service to others, He showed that "man shall not live by bread alone" (Matthew 4:4), but must be nourished by the word of God. He was "in all points tempted like as we are, yet without sin" (Hebrews 4:15), and so He is able to help those who are tempted (Hebrews 2:18).

He is the *Prince of Peace,* the ultimate *Comforter.* As such, He has power to comfort an anguished heart pierced by sorrow or sin. He provides a special kind of peace that no human agency can provide: "Peace I leave with you, my peace I give unto you: not as the world giveth, give I unto you. Let not your heart be troubled, neither let it be afraid." (John 14:27.)

He is the *Good Shepherd.* He possesses all the attributes of the divine nature of God. He is virtuous, patient, kind, long-suffering, gentle, meek, and charitable. If we are weak or deficient in any of these qualities, He stands willing to strengthen and compensate. This I know.

He is a *Wonderful Counselor.* Indeed, there is no human condition—be it suffering, incapacity, inadequacy, mental deficiency, or sin—that He cannot comprehend or to which His love will not reach out to the individual. He pleads today: "Come unto me, all ye that labour and are heavy laden, and I will give you rest." (Matthew 11:28.)

He is our *Advocate, Mediator,* and *Judge.* Because He is God, He is perfectly equitable with justice and mercy. He can simultaneously plead our cause and judge our destiny. Now let me describe to you what faith in Jesus Christ means.

Faith in Him is more than mere acknowledgment that He lives. It is more than professing belief.

Faith in Jesus Christ consists of complete reliance on Him. As God, He has infinite power, intelligence, and love. There is no human problem beyond His capacity to solve. Because He descended below all things, He knows how to help us rise above our daily difficulties.

Faith in Him means believing that even though we do not understand all things, He does. We, therefore, must look to Him "in every thought; doubt not, fear not." (Doctrine and Covenants 6:36.)

Faith in Him means trusting that He has all power over all men and all nations. There is no evil that He cannot arrest. All things are in His hands. This earth is His rightful dominion. Yet He permits evil so that we can make choices between good and evil.

His gospel is the perfect prescription for all human problems and social ills. But His gospel is effective only as it is applied in our lives. Therefore, we must "feast upon the words of Christ; for behold, the words of Christ will tell [us] all things what [we] should do." (Book of Mormon, 2 Nephi 32:3.)

Unless we *do* His teachings, we do not demonstrate faith in Him.

Think what a different world this would be if all mankind would do as He said: "Love the Lord thy God with all thy heart, and with all thy soul, and with all thy mind. . . . Thou shalt love thy neighbour as thyself." (Matthew 22:37, 39.)

What, then, is the answer to the question "What is to be done concerning the problems and dilemmas that individuals, communities, and nations face today?" Here is His simple prescription:

"Believe in God; believe that he is, and that he created all things, both in heaven and in earth; believe that he has *all* wisdom, and *all* power, both in heaven and in earth; believe that man doth not comprehend all things which the Lord can comprehend. . . . Believe that ye must repent of your sins and forsake them, and humble yourselves before God; and ask in sincerity of heart that he would forgive you; and now, if you believe all these things, *see that ye do them.*" (Mosiah 4:9-10; italics added.)

As members of the Church, we are

> *"under obligation to make*
> *the sinless Son of Man [our] ideal—*
> *the one perfect being*
> *who ever walked the earth.*
> *Sublimest Example of Nobility*
> *God-like in nature*
> *Perfect in his love*
> *Our Redeemer*
> *Our Savior*
> *The immaculate Son of our Eternal Father*
> *The Light, the Life, the Way."[1]*

With all my soul, I love Him.

He is the same loving, compassionate Lord today as when He walked the dusty roads of Palestine. He is close to His servants on this earth. He cares about and loves each of us today. Of this we can be assured.

He lives today as our Lord, our Master, our Savior, our Redeemer, and our God.

God bless us all to come unto Him, to believe in Him, to accept Him, to worship Him, and to fully trust in Him. This is my humble prayer, in the name of Jesus Christ.

David O. McKay, "Transforming Power of Faith in Christ," *Improvement Era,* June 1951, p. 478.